The **AA** **POCKET**Guide
EDINBURGH

Edinburgh: Regions and Best places to see

 Best places to see 30–51

 Featured sight

 Old Town 55–71

 New Town 82–97

 Canongate and Holyrood 72–81

 Around Edinburgh 98–115

Original text by Sally Roy

Updated by Hilary Weston and Jackie Staddon

© Automobile Association Developments Limited 2008. First published 2008

ISBN: 978-0-7495-5755-3

Published by AA Publishing, a trading name of Automobile Association Developments Limited, whose registered office is Fanum House, Basing View, Basingstoke, Hampshire RG21 4EA. Registered number 1878835.

Colour separation: Keenes, Andover
Printed and bound in Italy by Printer Trento S.r.l.
Front cover images: (t)AA; (b) AA/K Paterson
Back cover image: AA/J Beazley

A03604

 This product includes mapping data licensed from Ordnance Survey® with the permission of the Controller of Her Majesty's Stationery Office. © Crown copyright 2008. All rights reserved. Licence number 100021153. Transport map © Communicarta Ltd, UK

About this book

This book is divided into five sections.

Planning pages 16–29
Before you go; Getting there; Getting around; Being there

Best places to see pages 30–51
The unmissable highlights of any visit to Edinburgh

Exploring pages 52–115
The best places to visit in Edinburgh, organized by area

Excursions pages 116–129
Places to visit out of town

Maps pages 133–144
All map references are to the maps in the atlas section. For example, Arthur's Seat has the reference ✚ 141 D7 – indicating the page number and grid square in which it can be found

Contents

Planning

EDINBU
INSPIRING CAPIT

Before you go

WHEN TO GO

	JAN	FEB	MAR	APR	MAY	JUN	JUL	AUG	SEP	OCT	NOV	DEC
	4°C	4°C	6°C	9°C	12°C	16°C	17°C	16°C	15°C	12°C	7°C	5°C
	39°F	39°F	43°F	48°F	54°F	61°F	63°F	61°F	59°F	54°F	45°F	41°F

High season — Low season

Edinburgh experiences defined seasons. Spring (March to May) has a mixture of sunshine and showers although winter conditions can continue into March. May and early June are often the finest months with long clear sunny days but some chilly nights. June has long daylight hours but the end of the month is the start of the busy school holidays. The later summer months are less predictable with a fair chance of rain or thunderstorms. September is the official start of autumn but the season really starts in October when the colder days set in. Winter (December to February) can be cold, dreary and dark with the occasional bright frosty day to lighten the mood. Snow is a possibility but does not usually settle long in the city. For a five-day weather forecast visit www.bbc.co.uk/weather

WHAT YOU NEED

● Required
○ Suggested
▲ Not required

Some countries require a passport to remain valid for a minimum period (usually at least six months) beyond the date of entry – check before you travel.

	UK	Germany	USA	Netherlands	Spain
Passport	▲	●	●	●	●
Visa (Regulations can change – check before booking your journey)	▲	▲	▲	▲	▲
Onward or Return Ticket	▲	○	○	○	○
Health Inoculations	▲	▲	▲	▲	▲
Health Documentation (➤ 19, Health Insurance)	▲	●	●	●	●
Travel Insurance	○	○	○	○	○
Driving Licence (national)	●	●	●	●	●
Car Insurance Certificate (if own car)	▲	●	●	●	●
Car Registration Document (if own car)	▲	●	●	●	●

WEBSITES

- www.edinburgh.org
VisitScotland's dedicated website for Edinburgh and the Lothians
- www.visitscotland.com
Scotland's national tourism site

- www.edinburghguide.com
General information
- www.cac.org.uk
City of Edinburgh museums and galleries

TOURIST OFFICES AT HOME

In the UK

Scottish Booking and Info Centre
VisitScotland
Fairways Business Park
Deer Park Avenue, Livingston
Edinburgh EH54 8AF
☎ 0845 225 5121
www.edinburgh.org
info@visitscotland.com

In the USA

VisitBritain
551 Fifth Avenue, Suite 701
New York
NY 10176
☎ 1 800 462 2748
www.visitbritain.us
travelinfo@visitbritain.com

HEALTH INSURANCE

The National Health Service (NHS) provides free treatment for all EU nationals and residents of countries with which the UK has a reciprocal agreement – bring your European Health Insurance Card (EHIC) from your home country. Accident and emergency treatment is free to everyone. The 24-hour casualty department is at the Royal Infirmary of Edinburgh, 51 Little France, Old Dalkeith Road, Edinburgh EH16 4SA (☎ 0131 536 1000).

TIME DIFFERENCES

GMT
12 noon

Edinburgh
12 noon

Germany
1PM

USA (NY)
7AM

Netherlands
1PM

Spain
1PM

Like those in the rest of the UK, Scottish clocks go forward by one hour on the last weekend in March to give British Summer Time (BST). Clocks go back to rejoin Greenwich Mean Time (GMT) the last weekend in October.

NATIONAL HOLIDAYS

Scottish public holidays may vary from place to place and their dates from year to year; thus, although Edinburgh may be on holiday at certain times, other Scottish towns and cities will not necessarily be having a public holiday.

1 Jan *New Year's Day
2 Jan *Holiday
Mar/Apr *Good Friday, Easter Monday
First Mon May *May Day Bank Holiday
Mon, mid–late May Victoria Holiday

Last Mon in Aug August Bank Holiday
3rd Mon in Sep Autumn Holiday
25 Dec *Christmas Day
26 Dec *Boxing Day

* throughout Scotland

WHAT'S ON WHEN

January *Edinburgh Hogmanay:* This spectacular three-day street party, centred on Princes Street, has become Europe's biggest winter festival, with street theatre, ceilidhs and general merrymaking.

Burns Night Edinburgh celebrates the birthday of Scotland's national poet on 25 January, with traditional haggis dinners and draughts of whisky in hotels and restaurants all over the city.

April *Edinburgh Science Festival:* Lectures and events covering all branches of science and technology, held in over 40 venues city-wide.

May *Scottish International Children's Festival:* The largest festival of performing arts in the UK for children and young people.

June *Royal Highland Show:* Highlight of Scotland's country year, with a huge variety of events over five days, including pedigree livestock judging, show-jumping and agricultural displays.

August *Edinburgh International Festival:* Three weeks of top-quality opera, dance, music and theatre from all around the world, at a variety of locations throughout the city.

Edinburgh Festival Fringe: The world's largest arts festival, held over three weeks, with exhibitions, music, dance, comedy and shows for children.

Edinburgh Military Tattoo: A spectacular display of music, entertainment and theatre with a military theme, set against the stunning backdrop of Edinburgh Castle.

Edinburgh International Film Festival: The world's longest-running film festival has both mainstream and independent new releases, with interviews, discussions and debate.

Book Festival: An annual event since 1998, the festival occupies a tented village in Charlotte Square, and attracts a wide spectrum of authors.
Jazz and Blues Festival: The complete gamut of jazz forms can be found in the many venues that host this international festival.
September *Firework Concert:* A fantastic firework display against the backdrop of the Castle, accompanied by classical music.
Doors Open Day: Some of the finest private houses in Edinburgh are opened to members of the public on one day of the year; contact the Cockburn Association, Trunk's Close, 55 High Street EH1 1SR (☎ 0131 557 8686).
Mela: Scotland's biggest intercultural festival with colourful celebrations of music and dance, plus arts and crafts, and street performers.

Festival Booking
For information and reservations for Edinburgh festival events, contact:

Edinburgh International Festival
✉ The Hub, Castlehill, Royal Mile, Edinburgh EH1 2NE
☎ 0131 473 2000 (reservations); 0131 473 2099 (general information)
www.eif.co.uk

The Fringe
✉ The Fringe Office, 180 High Street, Royal Mile, Ediburgh EH1 1QS
☎ 0131 226 0026; www.edfringe.com

Edinburgh Military Tattoo
✉ Castle Esplanade, Edinburgh Castle
Tattoo Office: 32 Market Street, Ediburgh EH1 1QB
☎ 08707 555118; www.edinburgh-tattoo.co.uk

Edinburgh Film Festival
✉ Filmhouse, 88 Lothian Road, Edinburgh EH3 9BZ
☎ 0131 228 4051; www.edfilmfest.org.uk

Edinburgh Book Festival
✉ Charlotte Square Gardens, Edinburgh EH2 4DR
☎ 0845 373 5888 (box office); www.edbookfest.co.uk

Getting there

BY AIR

Edinburgh Airport

9.6km (6 miles) to city centre

🚋 N/A

🚌 30 minutes

🚗 20–30 minutes

Britain's national airline, British Airways (☎ 0870 850 9850), operates frequent scheduled flights in and out of Edinburgh; the airport is also served by BMI, Air France, Aer Lingus, KLM, Lufthansa, Ryanair and easyJet. Passengers arriving in Britain on intercontinental flights will normally have to route via London.

FROM EDINBURGH AIRPORT

Coaches Airlink operates a coach service to the heart of Edinburgh every 10 minutes on weekdays, less often at weekends and in the evening. The journey takes about 25 minutes and costs £5 return, £3 one-way. Tickets can be bought from the tourist information office inside the airport, from the ticket booth or on the bus. A map showing the route is available from the information desk and there is a map inside the bus. The route brings you in past the zoo and Murrayfield sports stadium, and goes along Princes Street to Waverley Bridge and the rail station. Buses, including all public buses, leave from the arrivals area in front of the terminal building.
Taxis Taxis wait outside the arrivals hall in the rank beside the coach park. The journey takes about 25 minutes and costs around £15.

ARRIVING BY RAIL

Edinburgh has two major rail stations: Edinburgh Haymarket and Edinburgh Waverley. Waverley is the central station for onward travel within Scotland. Internal services are run by First ScotRail (☎ 08457 55 00 33; www.firstscotrail.com). For details of fares and services on Britain's National Rail network contact the National Rail Enquiry Service (☎ 08457 484950; www.nationalrail.co.uk).

ARRIVING BY COACH

Coaches arrive from England, Wales and Scotland at the St Andrews Street bus station in Edinburgh. The main coach companies operating to and from here are National Express (☎ 08705 808080; www.nationalexpress.com) and Scottish Citylink (☎ 08705 505050; www.citylink.co.uk).

ARRIVING BY CAR

Driving in the city is difficult with its one-way systems, narrow streets, Red Routes (double and single red lines indicate that stopping to park, board or alight from a vehicle is prohibited) and dedicated bus routes. Limited on-street parking is mostly pay-and-display (from 8:30am to 6:30pm Monday–Saturday). There are designated parking areas, to the south of Princes Street; the biggest is at Greenside Place, off Leith Street.

Getting around

PUBLIC TRANSPORT

Internal Flights operate to Inverness, Kirkwall, Stornoway, Sumburgh, and Wick; also to Birmingham, Bristol, Cardiff, Exeter, Jersey, Lerwick, Leeds Bradford, London City, London Heathrow, London Gatwick, London Stansted, Manchester, Norwich and Southampton. For the Western Isles, fly from Glasgow Airport.

Trains Edinburgh has two mainline railway stations: Edinburgh Waverley and Edinburgh Haymarket. Most internal rail services are run by First ScotRail (☎ 08457 55 00 33; www.firstscotrail.com). For details of fares and services call the National Rail Enquiry Scheme (☎ 08457 484950; www.nationalrail.co.uk) or visit the information desk at Waverley Station.

Buses Coaches arrive in Edinburgh from England, Wales and all over Scotland at the St Andrew Square Bus Station; National Express (☎ 08705 808080, www.nationalexpress.com) is the main operator to and from England and Scottish Citylink (☎ 08705 505050; www.citylink. co.uk) is the main operator across Scotland. Other Scottish bus companies also operate into the terminal, which has an information office.

Boat Trips The *Maid of the Forth* leaves daily from Hawes Pier, South Queensferry, sailing beneath the Forth Rail Bridge to Inchcolm Island between Easter and October (☎ 0131 331 5000). From North Berwick, the *Sula II* sails two to four times daily around the Bass Rock between Easter and September (☎ 01620 892838).

Urban Transport Pay on boarding, ensure you have the correct fare. The chief Edinburgh operator is Lothian Buses (for general information ☎ 0131 555 63 63, www.lothianbuses.co.uk). Lothian Buses have three travel shops (27 Hanover Street, Shandwick Place and Waverley Bridge, Princes Street).

TAXIS

Edinburgh Airport Taxis (☎ 0131 344 3344/333 2255); city centre taxis are black and can be hailed on the street, picked up at ranks or you can call Computer Cabs (☎ 0131 228 2555) or City Cabs (☎ 0131 228 1211).

FARES AND TICKETS

Buses You need to pay on board and ensure you have the exact fare as no change is given. Put the money into the slot in front of the driver and take your ticket from the machine behind the driver. Standard adult fare for a single journey is £1. A flat-rate single journey at night (any distance) is £2.

A CitySingle costing £20 for 21 trips is available from Lothian travel shops (► 24). A child aged 5–15 pays 60p to travel any distance. You can buy a Dayticket from the driver for a day's unlimited travel (adult £2.30, child £2). Timetables and tickets are available at the Travel Shops. An enlarged map and timetable on the bridge outside Waverley Station has additional information about the night bus service into the suburbs.

Edinburgh Pass This card gives free access to more than 25 attractions in Edinburgh and the Lothians. It includes free bus travel, including airport bus transfer, and special offers from some shops, restaurants and Festival events. A free guidebook explains what's on offer. Cost: 1-day pass £20, 2-day £36 and 3-day £45. You can buy online at www.edinburgh.org/pass or from the Tourist Information Centres at the airport or in the city.

DRIVING
- Speed limit on motorways: 110kph (70mph).
- Speed limit on main roads: 100kph (60mph).
- Speed limit on minor roads: 50–65kph (30–40mph) advisable, and compulsory in built-up areas.
- Seatbelts must be worn in front and back seats at all times
- Random breath testing. Never drive under the influence of alcohol.
- Non-leaded, leaded and diesel fuel is available from all service stations. This normally comes in three grades, premium unleaded, 4-star and city diesel. Petrol stations are normally open 6am–10pm Monday–Saturday and 8am–8pm on Sundays, though some (often self-service) are open 24 hours. All take credit and direct debit cards and many have well-stocked shops.
- If you break down driving your own car you can call the AA and join on the spot if you are not already a member (☎ 0800 887766). If you are driving a rental car, call the emergency number given to you by the rental company; most rental firms provide a rescue service.

CAR RENTAL
Local firms include Arnold Clark (☎ 0131 607 4500), Edinburgh Self Drive (☎ 0131 229 8686) and Condor Self Drive (☎ 0131 229 6333). International rental firms such as Avis, Hertz and Budget have offices at Edinburgh Airport (☎ 08700 400 007).

Being there

TOURIST OFFICES

**Edinburgh and
Scotland Info Centre**
Princes Mall, 3 Princes
Street, EH12 2QP
☎ 0845 225 5121
www.edinburgh.org
www.visitscotland.com

**Edinburgh Airport
Tourist Info Desk**
Ingliston EH12 9DN
☎ 0870 040 0007

St Andrews
70 Market Street
Fife KY16 9NY
☎ 01334 472021

Glasgow
11 George Square G2
1DY ☎ 0141 566 0800

North Berwick
Quality Street EH39
4HJ ☎ 01620 892197

Peebles
23 High Street EH45
8AG ☎ 0870 608 0404

Stirling
41 Dumbarton Road
FK8 2LQ
☎ 01786 475019

MONEY

Scotland's currency is pounds sterling (£) issued by the three major
Scottish banks (the Bank of Scotland, the Royal Bank of Scotland and the
Clydesdale Bank) in notes of £1, £5, £10, £20, £50 and £100. Bank of
England notes are legal tender and all coins are issued by the Royal Mint;
there are 1p, 2p, 5p, 10p, 20p, 50p, £1 and £2 coins. You can exchange
foreign currency and travellers' cheques at banks and bureaux de change.

TIPS/GRATUITIES

Yes ✓ No ✗		
Restaurants (service not included)	✓	10–15%
Cafés/Bars (if table service)	✓	change
Tour guides	✓	£1–£2
Taxis	✓	10%
Porters (depending on amount of luggage)	✓	£1–£3
Chambermaids	✓	change
Theatre/cinema usherettes	✗	
Hairdressers	✓	10%
Cloakroom attendants	✓	change
Toilets	✓	change

POSTAL AND INTERNET SERVICES

Post offices are open 9am–5:30pm Monday–Friday and 9am–12:30pm Saturday; Edinburgh's main post office at the St James Centre is also open until 5:30pm on Saturday. For Royal Mail queries: Customer Services (☎ 0845 722 3344). You can buy stamps in gift shops, stores and supermarkets

Many hotels have internet access available for guests and main public libraries also have internert access. For internet cafés in Edinburgh try easyInternetcafé, 58 Rose Street, EH2 2YQ (☎ 0131 220 3577, 7:30am–10pm, £1 per 30 minutes) or Moviebank, 53 London Street, EH3 6LX (☎ 0131 557 1011, Mon–Sat 2–10, Sun 2–9, 3p per minute).

TELEPHONES

Public telephone boxes are operated by BT and other telephone companies. Calls can be made using credit cards, phone company credit cards, phone cards (available in units of £2, £5 and £10) and coins. Edinburgh code: 0131; operator: 100; directory enquiries: 118500.

International dialling codes
From Edinburgh to:
Germany: 00 49
USA and Canada: 00 1
Netherlands: 00 31

Emergency number
Police, fire, ambulance: 999

EMBASSIES AND CONSULATES

USA ☎ 09068 200290
Germany ☎ 0131 337 2323

Netherlands ☎ 0131 220 3226
Spain ☎ 0131 220 1843

HEALTH ADVICE

Dental Services Dental services are free only to UK citizens who fall into certain categories. For emergencies, there are two free walk-in dental clinics in Edinburgh: the Edinburgh Dental Institute, Level 7, Lauriston Building, 1 Lauriston Place (☎ 0131 536 4913) and the Western General Hospital, Crewe Road South (☎ 0131 537 1338).

Sun Advice Some summers can be hot – use sunscreen or cover up.

Drugs Prescription and non-prescription drugs and medicine are available from chemists (pharmacies), often distinguished by a green cross. Some supermarkets have a pharmacy shop within the store. A pharmacist can advise on treatment for simple complaints.

Safe Water Tap water in Edinburgh is safe and reasonably palatable; bottled water is widely available in bars, restaurants and food stores.

PERSONAL SAFETY

Policemen wear a peaked flat hat with a black-and-white chequered band; they are friendly and approachable and will give directions and information willingly. In most tourist areas the main danger is petty theft.

- Do not carry more cash than you need.
- Beware of pickpockets, particularly in the main tourist areas.
- Areas to avoid at night include backstreet and dockside areas of Leith, wynds leading off Royal Mile, the footpaths across The Meadows and some peripheral housing schemes.

Police assistance ☎ 999 from any call box for true emergencies only.

ELECTRICITY

The power supply in Edinburgh is 240 volts AC. Sockets accept three-pin plugs. North American visitors will need a transformer and adaptor for electrical appliances, European and Australasian visitors an adaptor only.

OPENING HOURS

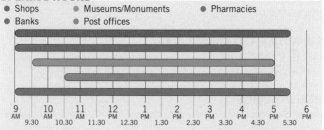

In addition, most shops in central Edinburgh are open until 8pm on Thursday and many open 12–5 on Sunday. Tourist-oriented shops are also open on Sunday all over the city, as is the Gyle Centre, a huge out-of-town shopping centre on the western outskirts. Some city-centre banks remain open until 5 or 5:30. Edinburgh has all-day licensing in its pubs and bars, which are normally open 11am–11pm or later.

LANGUAGE

You'll have no difficulty in understanding the people of Edinburgh, who tend automatically to modulate their accent when speaking to non-Scots. But there are many words and expressions that are uniquely Scots and used in everyday conversation, here are a few:

auld old; Edinburgh is often called Auld Reekie, a reference to its smoking chimney-pots which once cast a pall over the city

awfy very; a person might be described as 'awfy auld'

belong come from; an Edinburgh native says 'I belong tae Edinburgh'

ben mountain; Ben Nevis is the highest in Scotland and the UK

blether to chatter or a garrulous person; 'she's an awfy blether'

bonnie pretty, attractive; 'that's a bonnie blink' meaning an attractive view

brae slope or hillside

braw fine, 'he's a braw laddie'

burn stream

cairn a pile of stones, often on the top of a hill or acting as a memorial

ceilidh an informal gathering to tell stories and sing songs; now often an organized entertainment with a Scottish theme

clan Highland tribe or family group owing allegiance to a chief

couthy homey and comfortable

douce gentle and kind; can be used to describe weather conditions

dram a drink of whisky

dreich dreary, wet and dull; used about the weather but also about people and gatherings

first-foot the first visit paid to neighbours and friends after the start of New Year, traditionally with a bottle of whisky

fouter fiddle around

glen a Highland valley

gloaming dusk

guttered drunk

haar fine summer sea mist found on the east coast

harling mixture of limestone and gravel used to cover exterior house walls

hen affectionate and informal mode of address to a female

Hogmanay New Year's Eve

ken to know; either a fact or a person 'D'ye ken the High Street?', 'I dinnae ken Jock Fisher'

kirk church

laird estate landowner

lassie girl

lugs ears

lum chimney; as in 'lang may your lum reek' – ie good health

manse vicarage; the home of the minister

messages food shopping; 'I'm awa' tae get the messages'

policies grounds or parkland surrounding a substantial house

pend vaulted passage or archway

quaich a two-handled drinking bowl

sarnie sandwich

Sassenach originally a non-Gaelic speaking Lowlander, now usually a non-Scot

scunnered displeased, fed up

stay live; 'I stay in Edinburgh'

stravaig wander aimlessly, and pleasurably, about

stushie argument, fight

trews tartan trousers

wynd narrow lane between houses

Best places to see

1 Arthur's Seat

Edinburgh is unique in Europe in possessing a craggy peak within a stone's throw of the heart of the city, the perfect antidote to crowds and culture.

Holyrood Park (► 75) and Edinburgh itself are dominated by Arthur's Seat, the extinct volcano soaring 823ft (251m) above the city. The volcano erupted 325 million years ago during the early Carboniferous era; its other remnants make up the Castle Rock and Calton Hill (► 84). Geologists can trace the stages of today's rock formations – the summit marks where the cone erupted, while molten rocks formed the sills such as Salisbury Crags and Samson's Ribs. Erosion during the Ice Age laid bare the inside of the volcano, isolating the twin peaks of Arthur's Seat and the Crow Hill. Explanations for the name vary; some believe it to be a corruption of the Gaelic name for 'archers', others claim the Normans associated it with the semi-mythical King Arthur.

You can climb Arthur's Seat from a path starting near St Margaret's Well just inside the Palace of Holyroodhouse entrance to the park; the path divides at the start of Hunter's Bog valley and either branch leads to the summit. Take the right-hand one to go along the path called the Radical Road, which runs directly beneath the rockface of Salisbury Crags, or the left, through the Dasses, to the top. Easiest of all is to drive to the parking area near Dunsapie Loch; from here it's a short, steep climb to the top, with one or two rocky scrambles to give you a feeling of real achievement. However you get there, it's worth it for the panorama of the city, the Firth of Forth, the Pentland Hills and the coastline to the east of Edinburgh.

🚩 141 D7 ✉ Holyrood Park ☎ 0131 652 8150 (Historic Scotland Ranger Service) 🕐 Open access 🎫 Free 🚌 35 to palace entrance, other buses to perimeter ❓ No vehicular access, except to Dunsapie Loch on Sun

2 Edinburgh Castle

Redolent with 1,000 years of history, the courtyards and buildings of Edinburgh's main tourist attraction live up to its dominant position.

www.historic-scotland.gov.uk

Edinburgh Castle rises from an extinct volcanic outcrop at the top of the Royal Mile. From the Esplanade, used in August for the Military Tattoo, the 19th-century gatehouse gives access to the heart of the castle complex. In the 12th century St Margaret's Chapel was built by David I in memory of his mother, on the highest point of the Castle Rock. Around and below the chapel are the defensive batteries, and buildings such as the 1742 Governor's House, still used as the Governor's official residence, the Great Hall with its hammerbeam roof, and the Palace Block, a royal palace from the time of James I. Here, in 1566, Mary, Queen of Scots gave birth to James VI, who became James I of England. The Scottish Crown Jewels are the focal point of an exhibition telling their story and that of the Stone of Destiny, returned to Scotland from Westminster Abbey, where it had lain since 1296.

Explore the vaults known as the French Prisons below the Great

Hall; the name recalls their use in the Napoleonic Wars. Here, too, is the Prisons of War exhibition. On the ramparts is the siege gun known as Mons Meg, which was given to James II in 1457 and could fire a 267kg (608lb) stone nearly 3km (1.8 miles). Today, the only gun fired regularly from the castle is the daily 1 o'clock gun, echoing from the Mills Mount Battery.

🏛 138 B4 ✉ Edinburgh Castle, Castle Hill ☎ 0131 225 9846 🕐 Apr–Sep 9:30–6; Oct–Mar 9:30–5. Last ticket 45 mins before closing. Closed 25, 26 Dec; check for New Year 🖐 Expensive
🍴 Restaurant and café (£–££)
🚌 23, 27, 41, 42

3 National Museum of Scotland

www.nms.ac.uk

An eye-catching modern building houses more than 10,000 objects telling the story of Scotland's history, people, culture and achievements.

The National Museum of Scotland opened in 1998 as an extension of the old Royal Museum, itself a fine mixed collection of natural history and the decorative arts, housed in a Victorian building embellished with splendid cast-iron work. A new national museum for Scotland had been mooted since the early 1950s, and the finished complex provides the perfect foil for the superb collections within.

The museum is divided into seven main sections, each concentrating on a theme in the development of Scotland, and illustrating this through exhibits, display boards, and interactive information. From the geological formation of the landscape move on to wildlife and historical and modern land use, then to a section on early people, where a group of sculptures by Eduardo Paolozzi (b.1924) is decked with ancient jewellery and objects. The next level looks at the Kingdom of the Scots, the years between AD900 and 1701 when Scotland was an independent nation with a full cultural, social and religious life. Here you'll find the famous Lewis chess-pieces, carved from whalebone in the 12th century, the 8th-century Monymusk Reliquary, and the Bute Mazer, probaby made for Robert the Bruce. Later treasures include fine Scottish silver, glass and textiles. Moving on through displays showing the country's development after the Union with England until the Industrial Revolution, you come to the industries that made 19th-century Scotland the workshop of the world. The final level is devoted to sporting Scotland and a Scottish Sports Hall of Fame. The roof terrace gives fine views over the city.

✚ 139 C7 ✉ Chambers Street ☎ 0131 247 4422 🕔 Daily 10–5 Closed 25 Dec ✋ Free 🍴 Tower Restaurant ☎ 0131 225 3003 🕔 Daily 10am–11pm (££–£££), also two cafés (£–££) 🚌 2, 23, 27, 35, 41, 42 ❓ Regular lunchtime lectures; guided general and themed tours; free portable sound guide

4 National Gallery of Scotland

www.natgalscot.ac.uk

Superb Old Master and Scottish paintings, displayed in sumptuously decorated galleries, make the National Gallery a draw for all visitors.

Perhaps the greatest attraction of the National Gallery of Scotland is its size, for this comprehensive and high-quality collection can be enjoyed in a leisurely hour or two. Housed in a splendid Classical Revival building designed by William Playfair in 1848, it spans the history of European painting from the Italian Renaissance to French Impressionism. Many rooms are decorated to Playfair's original scheme, and contain fine examples of furniture contemporaneous with the artistic movements.

Italian Renaissance pictures include a lovely *Madonna and Child* by Verrocchio and Raphael's *Bridgwater Madonna*, part of the Duke of Sutherland's collection. The loan of this painting in 1946 helped the National Gallery to gain international significance. Northern Renaissance pictures include Hugo

van der Goes' Trinity altarpiece, commissioned in the 15th century for an Edinburgh church. Italy is represented by Titian and Tintoretto and Spain by El Greco and Velazquez – look for the superb and tactile picture entitled *An Old Woman Cooking Eggs*, where you can practically feel the eggshell. Works by French artists include Nicolas Poussin's cerebral and detached cycle of *The Seven Sacraments* (*c*1640), and some superb Impressionist pictures glowing with light. There are also German, Flemish and Dutch works, all of great quality.

Leave time to enjoy the Scottish collection, housed in an underground extension, built in the 1970s. This concentrates mainly on 18th- and 19th-century artists such as Allan Ramsay, Henry Raeburn and David Wilkie; Raeburn's engaging portrait, *The Reverend Robert Walker Skating*, is among the gallery's most popular pictures.

➕ 135 D5 ✉ The Mound
☎ 0131 624 6200;
recorded information 0131
332 2266 🕓 Fri–Wed
10–5, Thu 10–7; closed
25–26 Dec 💷 Free
🍴 Café, restaurant (£–££)
🚌 3, 10, 17 23, 27, 44.
Free bus links with all
five national galleries
❓ Lectures and changing
exhibitions

5 New Town

One of Europe's greatest examples of Georgian town planning, New Town combines crescents, squares and circuses into a harmonious whole.

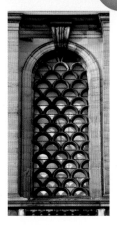

By the mid-18th century the crowded tenements and narrow streets of old Edinburgh were no longer adequate to house the population and institutions of the burgeoning city. A competition was launched with a view to building a fine 'New Town' to the north; the winning design was by James Craig and construction began in 1767. The Nor' Loch, on the site of Princes Street Gardens (► 92) was drained, and the North Bridge built to link the Old Town with the new. The first stage comprised three parallel streets, George, Queen and Princes (► 91), linking St Andrew Square (► 96) and Charlotte Square (► 86), the triumphant façades of the latter designed by Robert Adam in 1791. The more prosperous citizens flocked to live here necessitating further development. Robert Reid, William Playfair and James Gillespie Graham laid out the magnificent streets around Great King Street, the Royal Circus and Moray Place, a highly successful amalgam of interlinking crescents, octagons and ovals. This was followed between 1817 and 1860 by the construction of the West End, with Melville Crescent at its heart.

The result is the world's largest Georgian city development, with more than 11,000 listed properties. Happily, despite the appalling redevelopment of Princes Street in the 1960s, most has remained untouched. More than three-quarters of New Town houses are still in residential use, making the entire area an unchanged enclave.

🔹 135 D5 ✉ New Town 👹 Free 🍴 Restaurants, bars, pubs and cafés throughout the area (£–£££) 🚌 13, 19, 23, 27, 29, 37, 41, 42

6 Our Dynamic Earth

www.dynamicearth.co.uk

Edinburgh's Millennium Landmark project has brought a state-of-the-art attraction to Holyrood, the heart of devolved Scotland.

Against the backdrop of Salisbury Crags rises a light and airy structure, with a translucent spiked and tented roof, fronted by a sweeping stone amphitheatre. This is Our Dynamic Earth, an interactive museum telling the story of our planet using special effects and interactive technology.

A visit to Our Dynamic Earth lasts around 90 minutes and first concentrates on the creation of life; a 'time machine' takes you back to witness meteor showers, followed by the image of a barren, newly formed planet. Volcanoes erupt, the earth moves and shakes, sulphurous smells are all around and you can experience the cold of the polar extremes. Other areas concentrate on the evolution of life and the oceans, and you can visit a tropical rainforest, where the air is damp and full of squawks and chatters of unseen animals and birds. Every 15 minutes the sky darkens, lightning flashes, thunder roars and sheets of torrential rain pour down. In the FutureDome you can take your crew seat as a time traveller and discover what the future holds for our planet. Outside

you can take in Earthscape Scotland, an external gallery where you can do some fossil rubbing. This is also a great place to have a picnic.

The many interactive computer programs and information boards are suitable for younger children. There are dinosaurs and dodos, a submarine 'trip' to view ocean life, giant screens showing the glowing hues of the Northern Lights and much information on ecology, all presented with the emphasis very much on learning through fun.

➕ 137 D5 ✉ Holyrood Road, Holyrood ☎ 0131 550 7800 🕐 Apr–Jun, Sep–Oct daily 10–5; Jul–Aug daily 10–6; Nov–Mar Wed–Sun 10–5. Closed 24, 25 Dec. Last entry 70 mins before closing 🎫 Expensive 🍴 Café (£) 🚌 35, 36

7 Palace of Holyroodhouse

www.royal.gov.uk

The Queen's official Scottish residence, set against the background of Arthur's Seat, stands at the eastern end of the historic Royal Mile.

The Palace of Holyroodhouse is on the site of the original guest house for the medieval Holyrood Abbey, and is used today by Queen Elizabeth II as her home and office whenever she is in Edinburgh.

In 1501 James IV built a four-floor corner tower with gabled roof and balustrade, the existing northwest tower. Later additions were damaged and burned in 1544 and again in 1650. The palace attained its present form in 1671, when William Bruce designed an Italian-style courtyard quadrangle around which he built today's elegant structure. He fronted it by a tower matching the surviving medieval one, to which it is linked by an

entrance screen. The State Apartments, on the south side of the courtyard, include the Royal Dining Room, the Morning Drawing Room and the Throne Room. Across the court, the north range contains the Picture Gallery, decorated with portraits of 111 Scottish kings and queens from King Fergus in the 4th century to James VII, imaginatively created to order by Jacob de Wet.

Holyroodhouse has historical associations with many monarchs, among them James II, James IV and Charles II (whose canopied bed is on

show), while 'Bonnie' Prince Charlie held receptions here in the heady early days of the 1745 Jacobite Uprising. The memory of Mary, Queen of Scots is perhaps the most vivid; it was in her second-floor rooms that Mary's secretary, David Rizzio, was stabbed to death in 1566 by her second husband, Lord Darnley, and his conspirators.

✚ 137 C5 ✉ Canongate, Royal Mile ☎ 0131 556 5100 🕔 Apr–Oct 9:30–6; Nov–Mar 9:30–4:30. Last entry 45 mins before closing. Opening times may be subject to change at short notice – please telephone to check 💷 Expensive 🚌 35, 36 ❓ Winter exhibitions from the Royal Collections, Nov–Mar

8 Royal Botanic Garden

www.rbge.org.uk

The Royal Botanic Garden's collections of trees, shrubs and flowers are an oasis of quiet, and draw plantsmen and garden lovers from many countries.

The garden started life in 1670 with the founding of a Physic Garden near the Palace of Holyroodhouse; three centuries later the garden is a thriving and internationally famous plant study base, and a haven of colour and scent throughout the year.

Moved to its present site in 1823, the garden covers 69 acres (28ha) of undulating ground lying between the city centre and the Firth of Forth. Winding paths link the different sections of the garden, much of which is grassed and dotted with the superb trees that comprise the Arboretum, a

collection of more than 2,000 tree species, carpeted in spring with delicate spreads of bulbs. Spring flowers give way to rhododendrons and azaleas, their flaming reds and yellows offset by underplanting of lilies, primulas and *meconopsis*. The Rock Garden is at its best in late spring, its rocky slopes brilliant with Mediterranean and alpine plants, while the Heath Garden has year-round displays of Scottish and other heathers. High summer sees the 180-yard (165m) herbaceous border, with its stately beech hedge at its best, and the rose collections fill the air with scent. Horticulturalists will be fascinated by the Chinese Hillside garden, where wild plants clothe the slopes of a watery ravine leading to a pond.

The Royal Botanic Garden is particularly famous for its glasshouses, a complex of ten contrasting structures where you'll find everything from Amazonian rainforest plants to cacti from deserts all over the world. Don't miss the Temperate Palm House, an elegant cast-iron structure built in 1858, and still the tallest in Britain.

✚ *142 C4* ✉ 20A Inverleith Row ☎ 0131 552 7171
🕐 Apr–Sep 10–7; Mar, Oct 10–6; Nov–Feb 10–4
✋ Garden: free; glasshouses: moderate 🍴 Café and snack-bar (£–££) 🚌 8, 17, 23, 27

9 Royal Mile

Royal Mile runs downhill from Edinburgh Castle to Holyrood Palace and provides a focal point in the Old Town.

The vibrant, noisy streets of the Royal Mile are the tourist hub of Edinburgh. Thronged with people, lined with medieval tenements, packed with gift shops, and frequently echoing to the sounds of the pipes, this is the first port of call for every visitor. From the main thoroughfare, enticing closes and wynds (lanes) lead off between the buildings; discovering these is an essential part of exploring the Mile. Start at the top, where the solid bulk of the castle stands above the Esplanade with its splendid views, and work your way down to Holyrood, the historic full stop to an area crammed with history, described by author Daniel Defoe as 'the largest, longest and finest street…in the world'.

Starting from the Esplanade look for Ramsay Gardens, an 18th-century baronial complex at the top of Castlehill. Past the Tolbooth St John's Kirk, now the Edinburgh Festival Hub (▶ 60–61), fine 16th- and 17th-century tenements line The Lawnmarket (▶ 63). A nearby close was home to Deacon Brodie, this city worthy led a double life as a burglar and was hanged in 1788 outside St Giles' Cathedral (▶ 78), which stands at the top of the High Street. Opposite the cathedral, the City Chambers stand on the site of Mary King's Close, a medieval street which was blocked off during the Great Plague of 1645, its inhabitants left to die. Farther down, are more fine 16th-century buildings and a pub, the World's End, whose name commemorates the old city boundary.

Below the High Street the Mile becomes Canongate, named after the Augustinian monks whose monastery once stood here. High points include Canongate Kirk dating from 1688. More attractive houses herald the approach to the Scottish Parliament building and the Palace of Holyroodhouse (▶ 44–45).

DEACON BRODIES

🚹 139 B7 ✉ Royal Mile 🍴 Restaurants, bars, pubs and cafés (£–£££) 🚌 23, 27, 35, 41, 42

10 Scott Monument

www.cac.org.uk

Fine views to the castle and Princes Street from one of the most grandiose memorials to a writer ever built, make the climb well worth while.

Worn out with excessive work in an attempt to pay off his creditors and those of his bankrupt publishers and printers, Sir Walter Scott died at his home, Abbotsford, in 1832. He was regarded by his contemporaries as one of Scotland's greatest writers, and no time was lost in erecting a fitting monument to his genius. The architect was George Meikle Kemp, a self-taught draughtsman, who won a competition for the memorial's design in 1838. The 200ft (61m) monument went up between 1840 and 1846, a riot of ornate Gothicism with a seated statue of Scott beneath the central vault. In contrast to the sandstone of the building, the statue is carved from white Carrara marble, the block from which it was sculpted happily having survived falling into Livorno harbour on its way from Italy to Leith. Scott is shown draped in plaid, with his favourite deerhound, Maida. The monument's 64 niches contain statues that represent many of the characters from Scott's works – fans of the Waverley novels can identify their favourites.

Climb right to the top of the Monument for sweeping views over the city; your ticket price includes a certificate to prove that you really did it. If the prospect of the 287 steps seems rather

daunting, you could go as far as the first level only. Here you'll find a small room that displays information about Scott's life and work, and there are also headphones which you can use to listen to readings and musical settings of his novels.

✚ 135 D6 ✉ East Princes Street Gardens ☎ 0131 529 4068 ⏰ Apr–Sep Mon–Sat 9–6, Sun 10–6; Oct–Mar Mon–Sat 9–3, Sun 10–3 ✋ Moderate 🍴 Refreshment kiosk in East Princes Gardens (£) 🚌 23, 27, 41 and others to Princes Street

Exploring

For many Scots, the Edinburgh of today seems more like a true capital city than it has for almost 300 years, since it is now the place where the Scottish Parliament sits to determine issues affecting the country's people.

The city has enjoyed wonderful architecture and fine museums for many years; in this, the third millennium, it does so with a sound economy, growing prosperity and a clutch of new buildings and enterprises. It offers excellent exhibition and conference facilities, its financial institutions are of international importance and the research carried out in its universities is renowned worldwide. Increasingly a truly cosmopolitan city, with a cultural life whose dynamism is no longer confined to August and the Festival, Edinburgh rates highly for the quality of life enjoyed by its citizens and those who come to visit.

Old Town

This district epitomizes 'auld' Edinburgh, steeped in history and dominated by the formidable fortification, Edinburgh Castle.

Visit the castle to learn more of the history of the city and be sure not to miss it lit up at night. In the Old Town you can explore the tiny alleys known as wynds that branch out from the main thoroughfare, the Royal Mile, which stretches down to the Palace of Holyroodhouse. At the Old Town end this road is made up of Castlehill, Lawnmarket and the High Street with specialist shops, traditional pubs and a mix of cosmopolitan restaurants. This was the area where, until the building of the New Town in the 18th century, all classes of society lived cheek by jowl. After the new building the working classes were left to inhabit the tenement buildings and the narrow alleys, now seen as a historic visitor attraction.

CAMERA OBSCURA AND WORLD OF ILLUSIONS

The camera obscura, invented in the 19th century, uses mirrors to project images of the outside world on to lenses and thus to a white disk. The lenses rotate 360 degrees, giving a bird's-eye view. It's a fair climb up to Edinburgh's Camera Obscura, but you can pause at the hologram exhibition to get your breath. Go on a clear day as the camera depends on natural light and you won't see much if it's gloomy.

www.camera-obscura.co.uk

🏛 139 B5 ✉ Castlehill, Royal Mile ☎ 0131 226 3709 🕔 Apr–Oct daily 9:30–6 (later in high summer); Nov–Mar 10–5 ✋ Expensive 🚌 23, 27, 35, 41, 42

COWGATE

The long gloomy street called the Cowgate runs canyon-like beneath the South and George IV bridges, and connects The Grassmarket (➤ 62) with the Canongate area of the Old Town. Through here, in medieval times, cattle were driven from the plots behind the High Street houses to pasture outside the walls. By 1500 the Cowgate had become Edinburgh's first fashionable suburb, lined with the houses of rich merchants and the aristocracy. Centuries later, it housed Edinburgh's large Irish community and was home to the city's breweries. Look for **St Cecilia's Hall;** built in 1763, this was the city's first concert venue. The building of the new Scottish Parliament, and the opening of new bars and clubs revitalized the area and has compensated for the catastrophic fire that swept through Cowgate in 2002.

🏛 139 B7 ✉ Cowgate 🚌 8, 35, 41, 42

St Cecilia's Hall

✉ Cowgate ☎ 0131 650 2805 ❓ Concert venue for University of Edinburgh

EDINBURGH CASTLE

Best places to see, ➤ 34–35.

EDINBURGH CASTLE MUSEUMS

Besides its ramparts, batteries, courtyards and fine buildings, **Edinburgh Castle** (➤ 34–35) also houses an interesting museum, mainly connected with Scotland's military past. Though not strictly a museum, the Scottish National War Memorial draws thousands of visitors to admire its austere splendours. Designed by Robert Lorimer in 1924, it first commemorated the more than 100,000 Scots who died in World War I. Nearby is the **National War Museum of Scotland,** a military museum devoted to the uniforms and equipment of the armed forces in the country. Sections are devoted to the Royal Navy and the Royal Air Force. There are no less than nine Victoria Crosses on display, together with a mass of paintings, photos and general military ephemera as well as personal items and weapons. On the castle rampart is Mons Meg, a huge cannon built in Belgium and presented in the 15th century to James II as one of a pair.

Edinburgh Castle

🚼 138 B4 ✉ Edinburgh Castle, Castle Hill ☎ 0131 225 9846 🏙 ➤ 34–35 🖐 Expensive 🍴 Restaurant and café (£–££) 🚌 23, 27, 35, 41, 42

www.nms.ac.uk

National War Museum of Scotland

☎ 0131 227 4413 🏙 Apr–Oct daily 9:45–5:45; Nov–Mar daily 9:45–4:45 🖐 Included in castle entry

EDINBURGH EXCHANGE

It's well worth walking up the Lothian Road and along the West Approach Road to take a look at the £350-million-plus development known as the Edinburgh Exchange, the new financial district. The development plan was launched in 1988, after the construction of the palatial Sheraton Grand on what was then the rather run-down lower reaches of Lothian Road. Impressive buildings have gone up, grouped around the Edinburgh International Conference Centre, opened in 1995 and designed by Terry Farrell. Building continues but the existing monuments to late 20th-century commerce, all soaring brick, stone and glass, are impressive enough. Worth noticing are the Standard Life building on Lothian Road, with its fine gates and railings, and the impressive Scottish Widows building on Morrison Street.

✚ 138 C2 ⊠ Lothian Road and West Approach Road 🚌 1, 10, 11, 22

EDINBURGH'S FESTIVAL CENTRE –THE HUB

More than 50 years after the first Edinburgh Festival, and nearly 33 after moving into 'temporary' headquarters in summer 1999, the Festival offices finally moved into a purpose-designed suite in the magnificently converted Tolbooth at the top of the Royal Mile. The exterior, designed by Augustus Pugin for the Church of Scotland in the 1840s, remains unchanged, while inside you'll find some of Scotland's most exciting and innovative contemporary design. Sculptures, lighting, textiles and tiling make the mundane

act of buying a ticket part of the Festival experience. The Hub is open year-round and provides a 'taste of the Festival' no matter when you come, with information and tickets on all the city's festivals throughout the year (➤ 20–21), a hall and library, restaurant, shop and other facilities.

www.thehub-edinburgh.com

➕ 139 B6 ✉ Castle Hill, Royal Mile ☎ 0131 473 2015; Café Hub 0131 473 2067 🕐 8am–11pm 👆 Free 🍴 Café Hub (£–££) 🚌 23, 27, 35, 41, 42

GLADSTONE'S LAND

Gladstone's Land, a narrow, six-floor arcaded building and Edinburgh's finest surviving high-level tenement, was purchased in 1617 by Thomas Gledstanes, a merchant and burgess. He was a prosperous man, with enough money both to buy and decorate this sizeable and prestigiously sited building. Gledstanes remodelled the house, using the arcaded ground floor as a shop, and letting all but one of the other floors, which he retained for his own use. Today, the ground-floor booths display 17th-century wares, while the rooms on the first floor are furnished as the typical home of a wealthy citizen of that time. The main bedroom has a beautiful painted ceiling, decorated with fruit and flowers, and traces of the original frescoes on the walls.

www.nts.org.uk

➕ 139 B6 ✉ 477B Lawnmarket, Royal Mile ☎ 0131 226 5856 🕐 Apr–Jun, Sep–Oct, daily 10–5; Jul, Aug 10–7 👆 Moderate, but free to National Trust and National Trust for Scotland members 🚌 23, 27, 35, 41, 42

THE GRASSMARKET

Crouched below the Castle Rock, the long open space known as The Grassmarket is one of old Edinburgh's most attractive squares. With its cobbled pathways and groups of trees it has a French atmosphere and makes a pleasant place to pause for a little window shopping and a drink at one of its bars or pubs. It was first chartered as a market in 1477 and served for more than 300 years as the city's main corn and livestock market, besides being the site of the common gibbet. The Covenanters' Memorial commemorates the many citizens who were hanged here during the religious upheavals of the 17th century. The Grassmarket has been considerably smartened up in recent years, but manages to retain something of the atmosphere Robert Burns must have felt when he wrote *Ae Fond Kiss* in the White Hart Inn.

✚ 139 C5 ✉ The Grassmarket 🍴 Restaurants and cafés nearby (£–££)
🚌 2, 35, 41, 42

GREYFRIARS KIRK

Historic Greyfriars Kirk, standing on the site of a Franciscan friary, was built in 1620, a simple and peaceful church surrounded by a green kirkyard, the site of the signing of the National Covenant in 1638 (➤ 69). Most visitors come here to see the statue of a small Skye terrier on a fountain opposite the churchyard gate. The statue commemorates Greyfriars Bobby, a loyal dog who kept watch here at his master's grave for 14 years until his own death in 1872.

✚ 139 C6 ✉ 2 Greyfriars Place, Candlemaker Row ☎ 0131 226 5429
🕓 Easter–Oct Mon–Fri 10:30–4:30, Sat 10:30–2:30 ✋ Free 🚌 2, 23,
27, 35, 41, 42

THE HEART OF MIDLOTHIAN

Stand with your back to the entrance to St Giles' Cathedral and move about 20 paces forward and slightly to your right. At your feet you'll see the outline of a heart laid out in cobblestones. This is the Heart of Midlothian, which marks the place of the old

Tolbooth prison, where executions took place. In the past, locals would spit on the spot, although this no longer happens!

➕ 139 B6 ✉ High Street 🍴 Restaurants and cafés nearby (£–£££) 🚌 23, 27, 35, 41, 42

THE LAWNMARKET

The Lawnmarket is the name given to the section of the Royal Mile below Castlehill and above the High Street. It is one of the oldest streets in Edinburgh, and originally formed the 12th-century nucleus of David I's burgh. Its name comes from the 'lawn' or cloth once sold here and by the late 17th century it was the smartest place to live. Running off The Lawnmarket are some of the Old Town's best examples of closes and vennels. There are three entrances to James's Court, an 18th-century close, once the home of David Hume, the philosopher, and James Boswell, Dr Johnson's biographer. Milne's Court, to the west, went up in 1690, a planned development to try to ease the congestion in the Old Town. Look out, too, for Brodie's Close, home to the notorious Deacon Brodie.

➕ 139 B6 ✉ The Lawnmarket 🍴 Restaurants, pubs and cafés nearby (£–£££) 🚌 23, 27, 28, 35, 41, 42

THE MEADOWS

The open grassy space of Meadow Park is known as The
Meadows. Criss-crossed with paths and studded with trees,
it is popular with students from the university, doctors and nurses
from the nearby Royal Infirmary and families from the surrounding
residential streets. It's a good place to relax or let children run
about, and there's a playground with slides and swings. The
whole area was once covered by the Burgh Loch, which supplied
Edinburgh's water. Piped water arrived in 1676, the loch was
drained in the 18th century and The Meadows became a public
park in 1860. Twenty-six years later the grand International
Exhibition of Industry was held here; the Whalebone Arch is a
relic of this. Enjoy The Meadows by day, but its unlit paths are
better avoided at night.

✚ 139 E6 ✉ The Meadows 🚌 3, 3A, 5, 7, 31

MERCAT CROSS

Spare a few moments as you walk down Royal Mile to admire
the Mercat Cross outside St Giles. It is one of the most evocative
symbols of Edinburgh. Today's version dates from the 1880s and is
modelled on the 17th-century cross; it was restored in 1970 and
again in 1990, when the eight medallions showing the arms of
Britain, Scotland, England and Ireland and another four connected
with Edinburgh were gilded. In medieval times the Mercat Cross
was the focus for trade, and there's probably been a cross on this
site since the 12th century. Public festivities took place here, royal
proclamations were read, and executions performed. In 1513 the
troops set out from here on the fateful march to defeat at the
Battle of Flodden.

✚ 139 B7 ✉ High Street 🚌 23, 27, 35, 41, 42

NATIONAL MUSEUM OF SCOTLAND

Best places to see, ➤ 36–37.

PARLIAMENT HOUSE

From 1639 until the Treaty of Union in 1707 the Scots Parliament met in Parliament House, a superb 17th-century Scottish Renaissance building just behind St Giles' Cathedral. The long and lofty main chamber, Parliament Hall, was home to the 'Three Estates' – no distinction was made in Scotland between clergy, nobility and burgesses. Scottish MPs processed from here in July 1999 before the opening of the new Scottish Parliament Building (➤ 80). The hall has a magnificent hammerbeam roof and a fine 19th-century stained-glass window. The building is now occupied by law courts and advocates' chambers, and there's an interesting display on its history and present use.

 139 B7 ✉ Parliament Square ☎ 0131 225 2595 ⏱ Mon–Fri 9–5 🖐 Free
🚌 23, 27, 35, 41, 42

PARLIAMENT SQUARE

Parliament Square, lying behind St Giles' Cathedral, is an open space surrounded by the 19th-century colonnades masking Parliament House; they were designed by Robert Reid and built between 1803 and 1830. The equestrian statue of Charles II excited much comment when it went up in 1685, Roman triumphal dress being less than familiar to the locals. You'll see lawyers hurrying through the square on their way to the Court of Session and the High Court of Justice.

✚ 139 B7 ✉ Parliament Square 🚌 23, 27, 35, 41, 42

THE REAL MARY KING'S CLOSE

Beneath Royal Mile lies a warren of narrrow medieval streets, covered when the City Chambers were constructed during the 1750s. The houses along here had been tall tenements; some were knocked down to create space, others incorporated into the foundations of the City Chambers, the rest bricked up and forgotten. You can now explore this hidden world, guided by characters based on the people who lived there. The tour takes in some fine 17th-century houses, a sawmaker's shop and the home of a gravedigger where you find out about the 1644 plague.
www.realmarykingsclose.co.uk

✚ 139 A6 ✉ 2 Warriston's Close, High Street ☎ 08702 430160 🕐 Apr–Oct daily 10–9 (Aug 9–9); Nov–Mar Sun– Fri 10–4, Sat 10–9. Advance reservation rcommended 🖐 Expensive 🚌 23, 28, 35, 41, 42

ROYAL MILE

Best places to see, ➤ 48–49.

ST GILES' CATHEDRAL

St Giles' Cathedral, the High Kirk of Edinburgh, dark and
atmospheric, dates mainly from the 14th and 15th centuries.
The oldest parts of the church are the four massive columns
surrounding the Holy Table in the crossing; these support the
central lantern, with its flying buttresses and spire, raised in
1500. The original cruciform church was widened by the
construction of extra chapels; the choir, which dates to 1419,
is among the finest pieces of medieval architecture in Scotland.
Another highlight is the Thistle Chapel, an exquisite Gothic Revival
masterpiece designed by Robert Lorimer in 1909 for the Knights
of the chivalric Order of the Thistle. St Giles was John Knox's
church; here he preached until his death in 1572, struggling to
establish Presbyterianism as Scotland's faith during the reign

of Mary, Queen of Scots. Here too, the religious disturbances of 1637 began when the new Prayer Book, similar to the English Prayer Book, was introduced; this led to the signing of the National Covenant abolishing Episcopacy.

www.stgilescathedral.org.uk

✚ 139 B7 ✉ Parliament Square, High Street
☎ 0131 225 9442 🕐 Mon–Sat 9–5 (later in summer), Sun 1–5 💰 Free, donation for entrance to Thistle Chapel 🚌 23, 27, 28, 35, 41, 42

SCOTCH WHISKY HERITAGE CENTRE

Scotland's national drink is the theme of this entertaining and informative visitor centre, which attracts people from all over the world. If you want to learn about the history, manufacture and blending of whisky, head here. The introduction to the tour takes you through the different processes in the production of Scotch whisky. You'll learn about the different whisky regions and the effect of local conditions on the taste and 'nose' of the spirit, with a chance to have a sniff yourself. You'll meet the resident ghost, the Master Blender, then take a ride in a barrel-car through 300 years of whisky history, complete with scents and sounds.

www.whisky-heritage.co.uk
✚ 139 B5 ✉ 354 Castlehill, Royal Mile ☎ 0131 220 0441 🕐 May–Sep daily 9:30–6:30; Oct–Apr 10–6 (last tour 1 hour before closing) 💰 Expensive
🍴 Restaurant and bar (££)
🚌 23, 27, 35, 41, 42
❓ Tour includes free dram of whisky; around 270 varieties for sale in shop

TALBOT RICE GALLERY

The Talbot Rice Gallery, a huge and airy balconied building that opened in 1975, lies just off the Old Quad of the University of Edinburgh. It houses the Torrie Collection, a pleasing small collection of Dutch and Italian Old Masters. The gallery is probably better known for its changing exhibitions, which run all year round, with shows by established Scottish and other artists.
www.trg.ed.ac.uk

➕ 139 C7 ✉ Old College, South Bridge ☎ 0131 650 2210; 🕐 Tue–Sat 10–5; daily during Festival ✋ Free, but charges for some exhibitions 🚌 3, 7, 14, 33

UNIVERSITY OF EDINBURGH

The University of Edinburgh was founded in 1582. Its buildings are grouped around Old College, designed by Robert Adam in 1789. Nearby lies George Square, home to the arts and science departments, with a few fine Georgian houses still huddled beneath the monstrous 1960s campus building. The McEwan Hall is used for ceremonial occasions, while the Classical Reid Concert Hall also houses the Historic Instrument Collection. You can visit several of the university's buildings: The Playfair Library, one of Edinburgh's finest Classical interiors, is the pick of the bunch.

➕ 139 B7 ✉ University of Edinburgh Centre, 7–11 Nicolson Street ☎ 0131 650 2252 🕐 Mon–Fri 9:30–4:30. Closed Wed 12:30–1:30 ✋ Free 🚌 7, 8, 14, 33

VICTORIA STREET

The steep curve of Victoria Street links The Grassmarket with George IV Bridge and the Royal Mile. It's a cobbled street lined with some of Edinburgh's most individual and beguiling stores. As you walk down, look up to your right at the old tenements clinging to the slopes beneath Royal Mile. This area is the West Bow, once the processional way into the Old Town, and the former route from

Castlehill to The Grassmarket. Walk along Victoria Terrace, perched above the roofs of Victoria Street, to experience the atmosphere of this part of town.

✚ 139 B6 ✉ Victoria Street 🚌 23, 27, 35, 41, 42

THE WRITERS' MUSEUM

The Writers' Museum occupies a three-floor house on Lady Stair's Close, which was built in 1622 by a merchant whose daughter made it over to Lady Stair in 1719. (Lady Stair was the widow of the judge and Secretary of State John Dalrymple, 1st Earl of Stair, who was held largely responsible for the massacre of Glencoe.) The museum is devoted to Scotland's great trio – Robert Burns, Sir Walter Scott and Robert Louis Stevenson. There's much well-presented information on the lives and works of these writers in the form of memorabilia, documents and pictures, with sound guides to help you make the most of your visit. The museum also stages temporary exhibitions on aspects of the writers' lives.

www.cac.org.uk

✚ 139 B6 ✉ Lady Stair's Close, The Lawnmarket, Royal Mile ☎ 0131 529 4901 🕐 Mon–Sat 10–5; Sun during Edinburgh Festival 12–5 ✋ Free 🚌 23, 27, 35, 41 ❓ Changing temporary exhibitions on literary themes

Canongate and Holyrood

Canongate forms the eastern end of the Royal Mile. It gets its name from the Augustine monks or 'canons' who created a settlement close to the 12th-century Holyrood Abbey. Canongate was outside the walls of the city, relying on the sanctity of the abbey for protection.

Holyrood Park

The Canongate Tolbooth was the administrative headquarters of the borough until it became part of the city in 1856. This may not be the prettiest of Edinburgh's streets but it contains some of the best social history museums. At the bottom end of Canongate is the antithesis to these old buildings, the controversial and expensive Scottish Parliament Building. Behind this is another nod to modernity, the excellent Our Dynamic Earth science museum. Royal Mile culminates in the splendid Palace of Holyroodhouse, the Queen's official residence in Scotland. Beyond is the huge open space of Holyrood Park with Arthur's Seat at its heart, a wonderful area to walk and relax in after sightseeing.

ARTHUR'S SEAT
Best places to see, ➤ 32–33.

HOLYROOD ABBEY

You'll see the remains of the once-magnificent Holyrood Abbey, founded in 1128 by David I, on a visit to the Palace of Holyroodhouse (➤ 44–45). Legend tells that the king was thrown from his horse by a huge stag; while grappling with it he found a crucifix in his hands and later dreamed that he should found a monastery of the Holy Rood, or Cross, on the site. The present abbey was built for the Augustinians in the early 13th century, a cathedral-sized structure with a superb medieval façade. Burned by the English in 1544, partially destroyed after the Reformation, the Abbey was the scene of Charles I's coronation. In 1588 it was sacked by an Edinburgh mob, who desecrated the royal tombs, and in 1768 much of the remaining fabric collapsed.

✚ 137 D5 ✉ The Palace of Holyroodhouse ☎ 0131 556 5100 🕐 Apr–Oct 9:30–6; Nov–Mar 9:30–4:30. As the palace is a royal residence, opening times may be subject to change at short notice – telephone to check 🖑 Expensive 🚌 35, 36

HOLYROOD PARK

Once a royal hunting preserve, Holyrood Park, which includes Arthur's Seat (➤ 32–33), is unique among city parks. No other European city can boast a piece of wild countryside, complete with three lochs, dramatic cliffs and open moorland, within a stone's throw of its heart. You can escape to the park to picnic, walk, feed the ducks and geese or simply relax and do nothing. Queen's Drive, built at the instigation of Prince Albert, runs around the park and up towards Arthur's Seat; a pleasant drive, it's closed to all commercial vehicles. At its highest point you'll find Dunsapie Loch, another of Albert's inspirations. Don't miss St Margaret's Well, a medieval Gothic structure near Holyrood Palace where a clear spring wells from beneath sculpted vaulting.

✚ 141 C7 ✉ Holyrood Park ☎ 0131 652 8150 (Historic Scotland Ranger Service) 🕐 Open access, but no vehicular access on Sun (except to Dunsapie Loch) 🖑 Free 🚌 14, 21, 35, 44

JOHN KNOX HOUSE

Whether or not the key figure in Scotland's 16th-century Reformation actually died in the this building is open to debate, but the tradition was enough to prevent the destruction of this fine 1450 burgh house, all overhanging gables and picturesque windows. Today, it houses an exhibition on the complex subject of the Scottish Reformation, complete with an audio re-enactment of Knox's famous audience with Mary, Queen of Scots, when he condemned the Mass and her love of dancing. You can also learn about the house's other famous inhabitant, James Mossman, the goldsmith who made the Scottish crown. He was probably responsible for the lovely carved frieze on the exterior that reads: LOVE. GOD. ABVFE. AL. AND. YI. NYCHTBOVR. AS. YI. SELF. The house is also home to The Scottish Storytelling Centre.

✚ 136 D2 ✉ 43–45 High Street, Royal Mile ☎ 0131 556 9579 ⊘ Mon–Sat 10–6; Sun during Edinburgh Festival 12–6 ✋ Moderate 🍴 Café (£) 🚌 3, 7, 33, 35, 37

MUSEUM OF CHILDHOOD

The Museum of Childhood is a delight, its five galleries crammed with everything from train sets and tiddlywinks to teddies and tricycles. It started life in 1955 as the brainchild of town councillor Patrick Murray, who, right from the start, set his own distinctive mark on the vast range of exhibits – many

of the quirky and informative labels were written by him. Apart from the huge collection of toys from all over the world, many of them very old indeed, there are sections devoted to children's clothes, books, education, food and medicine. You can watch re-runs of old cartoons, listen to playground songs and children chanting multiplication tables and admire some truly palatial dolls' houses. The galleries echo with the cry 'I remember that' as grandparents, parents and kids rediscover the joys of childhood.

www.cac.org.uk

✚ 136 E2 ✉ 42 High Street, Royal Mile ☎ 0131 529 4142
🕐 Mon–Sat 10–5; Sun Jul–Aug 12–5 👋 Free 🚌 3, 7, 14, 33, 35

THE MUSEUM OF EDINBURGH

The three tenements comprising the Museum of Edinburgh, a warren of passages, crooked stairs and oddly shaped rooms, are as fascinating as the collections they house, which tell the history of Edinburgh. The building dates from 1570, and was home to merchants, aristocrats and working people at different times in its history; you can see how they lived in the room interiors scattered throughout. There's almost too much to see in one visit, with displays following Edinburgh's development from Roman times to the 19th century. The eclectic mix includes everything from silver to shop signs, but most visitors particularly enjoy the sight of Greyfriars Bobby's collar and bowl (➤ 62); while more serious-minded visitors shouldn't miss the 1638 National Covenant, signed by the Presbyterian leadership.

www.cac.org.uk

✚ 136 D3 ✉ Huntley House, 142 Canongate, Royal Mile ☎ 0131 529 4143 🕐 Mon–Sat 10–5; during Edinburgh Festival, Sun 12–5 🎫 Free 🚌 3, 7, 14, 33, 35

OUR DYNAMIC EARTH

Best places to see, ➤ 42–43.

PALACE OF HOLYROODHOUSE

Best places to see, ➤ 44–45.

THE PEOPLE'S STORY

For an insight into Edinburgh's social history pause on your way down the Royal Mile to visit The People's Story, a fascinating museum crammed with the minutiae of everyday life. There's a

wealth of objects and informative displays on everything from local bakers and brewers to tea rooms and pubs. The reconstructions of rooms provide a graphic illustration of the extent of Edinburgh's housing problems right into the 20th century.

www.cac.org.uk

✚ 136 D3 ✉ Canongate Tolbooth, 163 Canongate, Royal Mile ☎ 0131 529 4057 ⏱ Mon–Sat 10–5; Sun during Edinburgh Festival 12–5 ✋ Free 🚌 3, 7, 14, 33, 35

THE SCOTTISH PARLIAMENT BUILDING

Nearly 300 years after its last session, the Scottish Parliament opened once more in July 1999. First housed farther up the Royal Mile, in 2004 it finally moved into its permanent home at Holyrood. The architect, Enric Miralles, visualized the structure as 'sitting in the land', and the design and surrounding landscape reflect this. Architecturally, the building is a stunner, and so it should be, with the cost topping £400 million. The main focus is the Debating Chamber, an airy wood-and-steel, light-filled space. Four tower buildings contain committee and meeting rooms, and offices. You can explore the whole complex, learn more at the visitor's exhibition or attend a debate in the public galleries. The best time to visit is on non-business days when the chamber and committee rooms are open to the public.

www.scottish.parliament.uk

✚ 137 D5 ✉ Holyrood Road ☎ 0131 348 5200 ⊕ Business days (normally

Tue–Thu) 9–7; non-business days (usually Mon, Fri and weekdays when Parliament is in recess) Apr–Oct 10–6; Nov–Mar 10–4 🖐 Free; guided tours: moderate 🍴 Café (£) 🚌 35, 41 ❓ Tours: Sat–Sun 10:20–2:40; Nov–Mar Mon–Fri 10:20–2:40; Apr–Oct Mon–Fri 10:20–4:40; duration 1 hour, book in advance

THE TRON KIRK

Christ's Kirk at the Tron, a fine Palladian-Gothic church built between 1637 and 1663, got its name from the salt-tron, a public weighbeam, which stood outside. In 1785, the south aisle was demolished to make room for the bridges linking the Old and New Towns. Closed for worship since 1952, the Tron Kirk housed the Old Town Information Centre until 2006, but is at present closed awaiting its future.

✚ 136 E1 ✉ 122 High Street, Royal Mile ⏱ View from the outside only 🚌 3, 5, 14, 31, 35

New Town

When overcrowding in the Old Town reached crisis point in the mid-18th century, the great and the good of Edinburgh needed a solution. As a result of a competition to find the perfect 'new' town, the superb and elegant area of New Town was born. This was a far cry from the dark and dirty alleys and crowded tenements down by the castle. Space, grandeur and elegance were the order of the day.

One of the most remarkable observations about the city is how the Old and New towns sit side by side and yet are so incomparably diverse. Most visitors head straight for the castle and the Royal Mile but many stay in the New Town, with its townhouse hotels and pretty squares. The restaurants, bars and cafés of the streets behind the main thoroughfare, Princes Street, are buzzing by both day and night. A walk farther out will give breathing space and peace, a welcome break from the busy city centre.

ASSEMBLY ROOMS

Even if you're not attending a concert, the Assembly Rooms, opened in 1787, are well worth a quick visit. The plain façade, with its massive 1818 portico, leads to a series of elegantly proportioned rooms planned for equally elegant social occasions. The ballroom, 31yds (28m) by more than 14yds (13m), is lit by chandeliers; the music hall, even larger, is equally impressive. The Assembly Rooms are a key Festival venue.

www.assemblyroomsedinburgh.co.uk

✚ 135 C5 ✉ 54 George Street ☎ 0131 220 4348 ③ Check beforehand that the rooms have not been hired for a function 🖐 Varies for performances 🚌 24, 29, 42

CALTON HILL

A clutch of remarkable monuments adorns the slopes of Calton Hill (354ft/108m), another remnant of the volcano that formed Edinburgh's geological structure. The view from the hill's summit is splendid, with all Edinburgh spreading around, and vistas down the coast and across to Fife. For even wider views, climb the 143 steps to the top of **Nelson Monument,** built in 1807, and housing a timepiece in the shape of a white ball which drops from a mast each day at 1pm. Next to it looms the unfinished National Monument; modelled on the Parthenon in Athens, it was intended as a memorial to the Scots who fell in the Napoleonic Wars. Only 12 columns had been completed when the money ran out and it was known for years as 'Edinburgh's Disgrace'. The City Observatory, with its Gothic tower and astronomical dome, stands nearby; the grandiose Playfair Monument commemorates John Playfair, first president of the Astronomical Institution.

www.cac.org.uk

✚ 136 B3 ✉ Calton Hill 🚌 5, 45

Nelson Monument

✉ Calton Hill ☎ 0131 556 2716 ③ Apr–Sep Mon 1–6, Tue–Sat 10–6; Oct–Mar Mon–Sat 10–3 🖐 Moderate 🚌 5, 26, 33, 45

CHARLOTTE SQUARE

Charlotte Square, named after Queen
Charlotte, wife of George III, was designed
by Robert Adam in 1791 as part of the first
New Town (➤ 40–41). This triumphant
and harmonious example of symmetrical
architecture, with its central garden, was
planned to balance St Andrew Square at the
other end of George Street. The north and
south sides of the square present an unbroken
façade which hides the blocks' 11 individual
houses. The west side is occupied by West
Register House, originally St George's Church,
an impressive porticoed building topped
by a cupola. The square was intended for
residential use, though today many of the
buildings house offices. For a glimpse of
18th-century life head for the Georgian House
(➤ 88–89) on the north side.

✚ 134 D2 ⊠ Charlotte Square ❚❚ Restaurants, bars
and cafés nearby (£–££) 🚌 12, 19, 36, 37, 41

CITY ART CENTRE

The City Art Centre was established in 1980 in a building originally constructed in 1899, a splendid baroque edifice with an imaginatively converted interior. Its six galleries house the city's collection of Scottish art and provide space for a diverse range of temporary exhibitions – you're as likely to find a show devoted to *Star Wars* as to Michelangelo drawings or Egyptian antiquities. The permanent collection includes paintings, watercolours, photographs and sculpture. Look for works by William MacTaggart, J P Fergusson and Anne Redpath, all important 20th-century Edinburgh artists and members of the school known as the Scottish Colourists.

www.cac.org.uk

✚ 135 D7 ✉ 2 Market Street ☎ 0131 529 3993 🕐 Mon–Sat 10–5, Sun 12–5 👋 Free, but charge for entrance to major temporary exhibitions 🍴 Licensed café (£–££) 🚌 3, 3A, 31, 33, 36

GEORGE STREET

The central street of the three that form the grid of the first stage of the 1766 New Town, George Street has escaped the development that wrecked the architecture of Princes Street (➤ 91). This spacious thoroughfare, designed by James Craig and named after George III, is still liberally endowed with Georgian buildings, many of them housing prestigious businesses and smart shops. St Andrew's Church (1785), with its fine Corinthian portico, stands near the east end; it was here, in 1843, that dissenting ministers walked out of the General Assembly to found the Free Church of Scotland. Farther west, the Assembly Rooms (1787; ➤ 84) are worth a visit, while several of the opulent Victorian edifices which once housed banks have been transformed into elegant and lively wine bars, popular with Edinburgh's young professionals.

✚ 134 C4 ✉ George Street 🍴 Restaurants, bars and cafés (£–£££) 🚌 24, 29, 42

GEORGIAN HOUSE

The Georgian House, on the north side of Robert Adam's Charlotte
Square, offers a chance to see how Edinburgh's monied classes
lived in the grand houses of the New Town. Reconstruction of
the interior involved restoring the original decoration scheme,
weaving fabrics for curtains and coverings, and tracking down
contemporary furniture, rugs, paintings and fittings. You can see
the ground-floor dining room, laid up with Wedgwood and silver,
and, in true 18th-century style, a ground-floor bedroom, with
a dauntingly smart four-poster bed. The fashionably sparsely
furnished drawing room runs the full width of the house upstairs,
while the basement kitchen was the height of convenience in
Georgian times. It's crammed with utensils and dominated by
the huge range. Note the blue walls; it was believed that blue
kept the flies away.

www.nts.org.uk

⊞ 134 C2 ✉ 7 Charlotte Square ☎ 0131 226 3318 ⏲ Apr–Oct 10–5;

Mar, Nov–Dec 11–3 🖐 Moderate, but free to National Trust and National Trust for Scotland members 🍴 Restaurants, bars and cafés nearby (£–£££) 🚌 3, 12, 19, 36, 37, 41

HANOVER STREET

For one of the best views to be had in New Town, walk in either direction up and down the slopes of Hanover Street, the easternmost of the three streets crossing the grid pattern of the First New Town. To the south is the Classical façade of the Royal Scottish Academy, with the Mound, Assembly Hall and New College rising behind. To the north, the slopes drop away to give far views to the Firth of Forth and the Fife hills. The statue at the junction with George Street shows George IV, seemingly enjoying much the same vista.

✚ 135 C5 ✉ Hanover Street 🍴 Restaurants and cafés nearby (£–£££) 🚌 13, 23, 27, 28

THE MOUND

Until the 1760s the site now occupied by Princes Street Gardens was filled with an unlovely lake known as the Nor' Loch, created as a northern defence for the castle

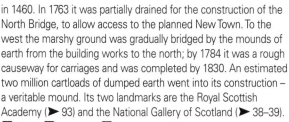

in 1460. In 1763 it was partially drained for the construction of the North Bridge, to allow access to the planned New Town. To the west the marshy ground was gradually bridged by the mounds of earth from the building works to the north; by 1784 it was a rough causeway for carriages and was completed by 1830. An estimated two million cartloads of dumped earth went into its construction – a veritable mound. Its two landmarks are the Royal Scottish Academy (▶ 93) and the National Gallery of Scotland (▶ 38–39).

✚ 135 D5 ✉ The Mound 🚌 23, 27, 41, 42

NATIONAL GALLERY OF SCOTLAND

Best places to see, ▶ 38–39.

NEW TOWN

Best places to see, ▶ 41–42.

PRINCES MALL (WAVERLEY MARKET)

Waverley Market, renamed Princes Mall, was opened in 1984
and occupies the site of the old vegetable market, which was
displaced in the 19th century by a market hall used for concerts
and exhibitions. This familiar landmark was demolished to make
way for today's functional granite structure, whose flat roof, level
with Princes Street, houses Edinburgh's main tourist office. The
specialty shopping mall, with more than 40 shops, is a good place
to hunt for more unusual clothes and gifts. There's a convenient
fast food area and a rooftop café, good for a quick lunch in
between sightseeing.

✚ 135 C7 ✉ Princes Street East End ☎ 0131 557 3759 ⏱ Mon–Wed, Fri,
Sat 8:30–6; Thu 8:30–7; Sun 11–5 🍴 Restaurants and cafés (£–££) 🚌 3, 8,
10, 17, 25, 27, 29

PRINCES STREET

Its situation alone makes Princes Street one of Europe's great thoroughfares, a straight and stately division between the Old Town and the New, with views south across Princes Street Gardens to the fabulous silhouette of the castle and Royal Mile. Lined with department and high street stores, Princes Street is where Edinburgh folk come to shop, and its streets are full of shoppers throughout the day. Built from 1769, it was named after George III's two sons. Princes Street once presented the elegant and harmonious face of restrained Georgian architecture, but deteriorated in the 19th and 20th centuries when dignified buildings were replaced with some architectural disasters. In the years ahead these will be replaced with elegant shopping and residential complexes, restoring some much-needed style to this superbly sited street.

✚ 134 D4 ✉ Princes Street 🍴 Cafés, bars and restaurants (£–££) 🚌 3, 10, 17, 25, 44 and many others

PRINCES STREET GARDENS

The green oasis of Princes Street Gardens occupies the site of the old Nor' Loch (➤ 89), drained during the construction of the New Town. The 8ha (20-acre) West Gardens, laid out in 1816–20 for the Princes Street inhabitants, are separated from the 3ha (7.5-acre) East Garden by the Royal Scottish Academy (➤ 93); both gardens became a much-loved public park in 1876. They are laid out conventionally and attractively with specimen trees, sweeping lawns and riotously bright planting. Children will love the Floral Clock in the West Garden, planted every year on a different theme; watch out for the cuckoo when the hour strikes. The gardens are edged with statues, which include the explorer David Livingstone, and James Young Simpson, the pioneer of the safe use of chloroform.

✚ 134 D4 ✉ Princes Street
🍴 Snack bars and kiosks in gardens
(£) 🚌 3, 10, 17, 25, 44 and others

QUEEN STREET

Queen Street runs parallel with Princes Street (➤ 91) and George Street (➤ 87), a long stretch of fine Georgian architecture largely untouched by modern development. The street, built between 1769 and 1792, was named after Queen Charlotte, wife of George III. Most of its buildings now house offices, but the fine views towards the Firth of Forth remain unchanged, as do the private gardens along the north side. James Young Simpson, the pioneer of anaesthesia, conducted his experiments on himself inside No 52.

✚ 134 C3 ✉ Queen Street 🍴 Restaurants and cafés nearby 🚌 8, 23, 27, 42

ROYAL SCOTTISH ACADEMY

This lovely Classical building, designed by William Playfair in

1822, is a fitting home for Scotland's Royal Academy, which moved here permanently in 1910. The Academy, founded in 1826, is based loosely on London's Royal Academy, and has both Academicians and Associates. It is at the forefront of art promotion in Scotland and to this end holds two major exhibitions annually; the Students' Art Exhibition and the Annual Exhibition. The Academy also lets the building to other arts organizations, such as the Royal Scottish Society of Painters in Watercolour and the Society of Scottish Artists, who stage their shows in the spacious galleries. It is also an important Festival exhibition venue, when its steps are thronged with Festival-goers enjoying street performances in the square outside.

www.royalscottishacademy.org

✚ 135 D5 ✉ The Mound ☎ 0131 225 6671 🕐 Fri–Wed 10–5, Thu 10–7
🖐 Varies according to exhibition 🚌 3, 23, 27, 41, 42

a walk around the New Town and Princes Street

Walk down North Charlotte Street and cross Queen Street to continue down Forres Street to Moray Place. Turn right and exit into Darnaway Street and along to Heriot Row. Continue along Heriot Row and cross the top of Howe Street to look at No 17 Heriot Row.

As you walk along Heriot Row, Queen Street Gardens are on your right; these were part of New Town's original plan to give householders access to green space. No 17 Heriot Row was the childhood home of author Robert Louis Stevenson; look out for the plaque beside the front door.

Retrace your steps to turn right down Howe Street then right again on to Northumberland Street. Where it meets Dundas Street turn right uphill, crossing Heriot Row and Queen Street to continue uphill on Hanover Street. Take the first right into Thistle Street and walk along to Frederick Street.

Thistle Street is one of the New Town's hidden and seductive shopping streets, where you'll find antique jewellers, elegant clothes shops and attractive cafés.

Turn left uphill, cross George Street and continue down to Princes Street. Turn left and cross the road.

You could take this opportunity to climb the Scott Monument (➤ 50–51) or visit the Royal Scottish Academy (➤ 93) or the National Gallery of Scotland (➤ 38–39), which stands just behind it.

With your back to the castle turn left along Princes Street or walk through Princes Street Gardens (➤ 92). At the end of the gardens, cross Princes Street and go straight ahead up South Charlotte Street.

Distance 2.5 miles (4km)
Time 1.5 hours walking; 4 hours with stops for visits
Start/end point Charlotte Square ✚ 134 D2 🚌 3, 12, 19, 36, 37, 41
Lunch Urbanangel (£) ✉ 121 Hanover Street ☎ 0131 225 6215

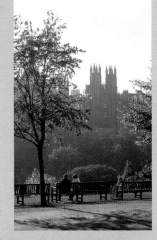

ST ANDREW SQUARE

Edinburgh's financial heart, St Andrew Square, lies
at the east end of George Street, and acts as the
architectural counterbalance to Charlotte Square at
the west end. Its design, dating from 1767, is not as
instantly pleasing. The grandiose mansion on the
east side, built in 1772 for Sir Laurence Dundas,
now houses the headquarters of the Royal Bank
of Scotland; another Dundas, Henry, 1st Earl of
Melville, surveys much of the New Town from the
central column. On the northeast side is Multrees
Walk, a prestigious shopping mall fronted by Harvey
Nichols' stylish department store.

✚ 135 C6 ⊠ St Andrew Square 🍴 Range of restaurants,
bars and cafés (£–£££) 🚌 8, 12, 17, 26, 29

SCOTT MONUMENT

Best places to see, ➤ 50–51.

SCOTTISH NATIONAL PORTRAIT GALLERY

The imposing red sandstone bulk of the Scottish
National Portrait Gallery looms over the east end
of Queen Street. Built in the 1880s, it's worth a visit
for the interior alone, with its wonderful arcaded
entrance hall glittering with lustrous murals. The
entire collection is devoted to the Scots, though not
all the portraits are *by* Scots. You can trace the flow
of Scottish history and achievement through this
diverse collection, though most people head straight
for Mary, Queen of Scots, Nasmyth's portrait of
Robert Burns and Raeburn's *Sir Walter Scott*.
Modern Scots to look for include Jean Muir, the
fashion designer, Sean Connery, alias James Bond,
and Irvine Welsh, the author of *Trainspotting*.

www.natgalscot.ac.uk

🚩 135 B6 ✉ 1 Queen Street ☎ 0131 624 6200;
🕐 Fri–Wed 10–5, Thu 10–7 🎟 Free 🍽 Queen Street
Café (£–££) 🚌 8, 10, 12, 16, 23, 27 ❓ Charges for
special exhibitions

WATERLOO PLACE

Waterloo Place is the continuation of Princes
Street to the east, a superbly balanced example
of grandiose neoclassical architectural design.
If you're hurrying through on your way to Calton
Hill, pause to admire the rhythm of the soaring
façades of its buildings. Waterloo Place runs
through the Old Calton cemetery; here are
buried some of the major figures of the Scottish
Enlightenment such as the philosopher David
Hume, and there's a fine view back to the castle.
More prosaically, the bottom of the place gives
access to the St James Centre, a hideous
blocklike concrete structure housing a wide
range of shops. The public outcry following its
construction probably did more than anything else
to further the cause of conservation during the
early 1970s.

Some scenes from the cult film *Trainspotting*
(1995) were shot in Edinburgh, where the action
is set, though most locations are in Glasgow.
Look out for Pivo Caffe near Waterloo Place;
this is where Renton runs into a car in the
opening scene. *Shallow Grave* (1995), from
the same production team, was also partly
filmed in the city.

🚩 135 C8 ✉ Waterloo Place 🍽 Bars and cafés (£)
🚌 7, 8, 14, 22, 29

Around Edinburgh

It's certainly worth looking beyond the city centre when making a visit to Edinburgh. Within a short bus ride or a reasonable walk there are some lovely leafy suburbs, as well as parks and small villages.

Cramond
Leith
Murrayfield
EDINBURGH
Musselburgh
Morningside
Swanston

Walking a little to the north, but still in New Town, are the charming streets of Stockbridge, with good restaurants and shops. To the west is Dean with its art galleries and the spectacular Water of Leith. To the south of the city is the gentle suburb of Morningside and just to the southeast is the village of Duddingston. A bus ride to the west brings you to Murrayfield and also to the excellent Edinburgh Zoo. Two miles (3.2km) to the north and easily accessible by bus is the old docks area of Leith, now gentrified with trendy restaurants, a huge shopping mall and the Royal Yacht *Britannia*. These are just a few of the choices, so take your pick and explore.

ANN STREET

The early 19th-century construction of the Raeburn Estate, built between New Town (➤ 40–41) and the residential district of Stockbridge at the bottom of the slopes of New Town, was instrumental in bringing new wealth down the hill as the rich moved in, occupying roads such as Ann Street. Now one of Edinburgh's most exclusive addresses, its attraction lies in its scale, almost miniature compared to the grandeur of the New Town. Each house in this classically inspired terrace of perfectly proportioned houses is fronted by a garden, producing a beguiling mix of small-scale architectural splendour and cottagey charm.

✚ *142 C4* ✉ Ann Street 🚌 29, 37, 41, 42

BLACKFORD HILL

Blackford Hill, south of the middle of the city, is seen at its best on uncrowded weekdays, and is a good place to head for an afternoon's fresh air and exercise and some splendid city views. Its 164m (538ft) summit is an easy climb from the surrounding parkland, up grassy slopes covered with bright yellow gorse. From here, the green southern suburbs stretch north, with Arthur's Seat over to the right and Edinburgh Castle ahead. You'll also find the Royal Observatory Edinburgh (➤ 109) on Blackford Hill. Head downhill to the wooded path that winds beside the Braid Burn to a castellated 18th-century villa known as the Hermitage of Braid. It is now a countryside information office which will fill you in on the surprisingly wide range of wildlife to be found in the area.

✚ *142 E5* ✉ Blackford 🚌 24, 38, 41

BRAID HILLS

If you're fit, you could combine a walk on Blackford Hill with a few more miles over the Braid Hills (205m/267ft) which lie just to the south and are linked to Blackford by good paths. Much of the area is covered by golf courses; these were laid out by the City of Edinburgh in 1889 as public courses when play on central

Bruntsfield Links was becoming restricted. Few tourists penetrate these outer hills, outliers of the Pentlands, and the only people you're likely to meet are local golfers and dog-walkers. There are more sweeping panoramas from Braid; on a clear day look north and to your left for a fine view of the Forth Bridges.

✚ *142 E4* ✉ Braid Hills 🚌 24, 38, 41

THE COLONIES

Downstream from Stockbridge, the Water of Leith walkway (➤ 153) will lead to you to one of Edinburgh's more picturesque

corners, a quiet cluster of streets of artisans' houses tucked away at the foot of the New Town heights. Here you will find the 11 parallel rows of terraced houses known as The Colonies, running at right angles to the Water of Leith. This development was constructed by the Edinburgh Co-operative Building Company in 1861 for local workmen and their families. Each house is divided into upper and lower dwellings, with outside stairs to the top flats and tiny gardens. Many of the houses are decorated with plaques depicting the tools used by the tradesmen involved in their construction – masons, plumbers, joiners, plasterers and decorators.

✚ *142 C4* ✉ Stockbridge 🚌 29

CRAIGMILLAR CASTLE

You'll have to brave some of Edinburgh's poorer housing schemes to reach Craigmillar Castle, one of Scotland's most impressive medieval remains, standing in fields on the southeast side of the city. The L-plan tower dates from the mid- to late 15th century and stands in a courtyard surrounded by curtain walls complete with massive corner towers. The castle was a favourite with Mary, Queen of Scots, and one of the two barrel-vaulted chambers is known as Queen Mary's Room. She fled to Craigmillar, 'wishing herself dead', after the murder of her secretary and favourite, David Rizzio, at Holyrood in 1566. Craigmillar later passed to the Gilmour family, who placed it in state care in 1946. Most children enjoy its empty spaces more than the packed precincts of Edinburgh's other, more famous castle.
www.historic-scotland.gov.uk

✚ *143 E6* ✉ Craigmillar Castle Road ☎ 0131 661 4445 🕓 Apr–Sep daily 9:30–5:30; Oct–Mar Sat–Wed 9:30–4:30 👋 Moderate 🚌 2, 14

CRAMOND

For a change from city sights, it's well worth making the short journey out to Cramond, a picturesque suburb on the shores of the Firth of Forth to the northwest of the city. Cramond was founded by the Romans, who established a harbour at the mouth of the

River Almond in the 2nd century as a base for the soldiers who were constructing the Antonine Wall. Sections of the Roman fort, including a well-preserved bath-house, have been excavated, and an impressive Roman sculpture of a lion was found near the water's edge in 1997. Cramond has attractive 16th-century houses, some later, more elegant, villas, an old and famous inn and a lovely cruciform church, built in 1656. During the 18th century, Cramond's river position led to the establishment of four iron mills along the Almond; Scotland's first commercially produced steel came from here.

Today, you can follow the River Almond Walkway upriver or walk beside the shore of the Firth of Forth. Offshore lies Cramond Island, a grassy tidal island accessible at low tide if you don't mind scrambling over the slippery rocks and blocks of the causeway. Across the river lies **Dalmeny House**, once linked to Cramond by a 450-year-old ferry service, which has miles of parkland walks (accessible July and August) and a delightful shore walk to South Queensferry (accessible all year). On your way back into the city, **Lauriston Castle** is worth a visit; this 16th-century tower house,

built for Sir Archibold Napier, was extended in the 1820s and has some fine Edwardian interiors reflecting the wealth of middle-class collectors of the period.

✚ *142 C2*

Dalmeny House

✉ Cramond ☎ 0131 331 1888 ⏱ Park: unlimited access all year 🚌 40, 41

Lauriston Castle

✉ Cramond Road South, Davidson's Mains ☎ 0131 336 2060; www.cac.org.uk ⏱ Apr–Oct Sat–Thu, tours 11:20–4:20; Nov–Mar Sat–Sun, tours at 2:20 and 3:20 ✋ Expensive (free access to grounds) 🚌 21, 24, 41 ❓ Many indoor and outdoor events between spring and Christmas. Full details from Lauriston Castle

DEAN VILLAGE

Thomas Telford's Dean Bridge spans the steep gorge of the Water of Leith, marking the northern limit of the New Town. Lying 105ft (32m) below the bridge is Dean Village, a quiet and historic enclave with attractive old houses and easy access to the river. In medieval times the Dean was Edinburgh's milling area, with 11 mills operating. Several 19th-century mill buildings survive, now converted into apartments – look for Well Court, originally built as housing for workers in 1884. Baxter's Tolbooth is a 17th-century granary. Across the river Dean Cemetery overlooks the village. This 19th-century graveyard contains some of Edinburgh's finest funerary monuments, the best of them designed by William Playfair, the New Town architect, who is also buried here.

➕ *142 D4* ✉ Dean Village 🍴 Restaurants and bars (£–£££) 🚌 19, 37, 41

DUDDINGSTON

Crouched in the shadow of Arthur's Seat, the ancient settlement of Duddingston is one of Edinburgh's most attractive corners. Its pretty streets run down to Duddingston Loch, now part of a bird sanctuary and always thronged with geese and other wildfowl. This is the loch purportedly featured in the National Gallery's famous picture of the Reverend Walker skating (➤ 39).

Duddingston Kirk is a 12th-century foundation, still retaining its Norman doorway and beautifully set in a verdant churchyard. Take time to wander around before heading for a drink in the Sheep Heid Inn, dating from at least 1580 when it was patronized by James VI; it has the oldest skittle alley in Scotland.

➕ *143 D6* ✉ Duddingston 🍴 Sheep Heid Inn (£–££) 🚌 44

EDINBURGH ZOO

Spreading up the slopes of Corstorphine Hill, Edinburgh Zoo is the headquarters of the Royal Scottish Zoological Society, with a strong accent on conservation, captive breeding of endangered species and education. With more than 1,000 animals from all over the world, plenty of hands-on opportunities and activities of all kinds, the zoo is child-friendly, and kids will enjoy the chance to see rhinoceros, bears, giraffes, zebras, hippos and many more. The well-designed lion enclosure is popular, and there's the Magic Forest, devoted to small rainforest monkeys. The highlight for most visitors is the daily penguin parade at 2:15pm; the zoo has a tradition of successful breeding of four species of these charming birds, which you can see swimming underwater through the glass windows of their pool. Be prepared to climb – the hill is steep.

www.edinburghzoo.org.uk

🚩 142 D3 ⊠ Murrayfield ☎ 0131 334 9171 🕐 Apr–Sep, daily 9–6; Oct and Mar daily 9–5; Nov–Feb daily 9–4:30 ✋ Expensive 🍴 Cafés and kiosks (£–££) 🚌 12, 26 ❓ Many special events aimed specifically at children

LEITH

There's been less-than-friendly rivalry between Leith and Edinburgh over the centuries, dating from the days when the latter controlled all Leith's foreign trade – indeed, Leith was only amalgamated with the capital in 1920. Its history as a dock area dates from before the 14th century, though its existing docks and warehouses mainly went up in the 1800s. Leith's dock area now boasts Ocean Terminal, Europe's largest shopping and leisure development, with three floors of shops, bars and restaurants, and a multiscreen cinema. This is one more sign of Leith's regeneration over recent years. Making a trip by bus down

Leith Walk, which links it to the city, is a good option for a change of pace, although it is rather run-down these days.

Head first for the Shore, a restored area by the Water of Leith, with desirable flats and excellent bars and restaurants. Nearby warehouses have been converted to smart accommodation; you can see these on Commercial Street, which gives access to the quay where the Royal Yacht *Britannia* (➤ 110) is moored. The impressive postmodern building housing the Scottish Office also draws the eye. East of the Shore several older buildings have survived near the Kirkgate, the old town area, spoiled by a disastrous shopping arcade and high-rise apartments. Leith Links lies farther east again, a pleasant green space much enjoyed by local dogs. The Links claims to be one of the earliest homes of golf; the ground was in use for golf in 1593 and it was here that the first set of rules was formulated.

✚ *143 B6* ✉ Leith 🍴 Restaurants, cafés and bars (£–£££) 🚌 1, 11, 22, 34, 35, 36

MORNINGSIDE

Tucked away in the quiet, leafy streets of Morningside on the southwest side of Edinburgh are solid Victorian villas still housing the prosperous citizens of Edinburgh's middle classes. Morningside, its respectability the butt of countless jokes, is one of several suburbs developed in the 19th century for the growing bourgeoisie, who wanted to live neither in the cold grandeur of the New Town nor the increasing squalor of the Old. The area is approached via 'Holy Corner', the affectionate local name for a crossroads surrounded by no less than four churches. Morningside, with its good shops, services and local amenities, has all a suburb could wish for; a stroll round here provides that insight into local life which is often so hard to find in major cities.

✚ *142 E4* ✉ Morningside 🍴 Restaurants, pubs and cafés (£–£££) 🚌 5, 11, 16, 17, 23

MURRAYFIELD

The western suburb of Murrayfield, all terraces and villas, was developed around 18th-century Murrayfield House in the 1860s. It's a well-to-do area with good local amenities and easy access both to the city and Corstorphine Hill. Twice a year Murrayfield comes into its own as crowds pour into Murrayfield Stadium, home of Scotland's international rugby union team, where home games are played during the Six Nations championship. The stadium, extended and modernised over the years, was built in 1925 by the then Scottish Football Union. The first game was played in March that year – Scotland beat England 14–11.

✚ *142 D3* ✉ Murrayfield ☎ Murrayfield Stadium 0131 346 5000 🚌 12, 26, 31

ROYAL BOTANIC GARDEN

Best places to see, ➤ 46–47.

ROYAL OBSERVATORY EDINBURGH

The Royal Observatory Edinburgh moved from Calton Hill (➤ 84) in 1895 when light pollution was starting to interfere with observations from the central site. This is still very much a working observatory, charged with the task of collating material for astronomers worldwide from the UK's telescopes here and overseas, and housing sophisticated equipment. The excellent visitor facility opens for pre-booked group vists and special events. The roof terrace has far-reaching views north to the heart of the city; if you're in Edinburgh during the winter, there are weekly Friday-evening viewing sessions at the observatory and a varied programme of winter talks starts each October.

www.roe.ac.uk

➕ *143 E5* ✉ Blackford Hill ☎ 0131 668 8404 🕐 Observing evenings: 7pm–8:45pm, booking essential 💷 Moderate 🚌 24, 38, 41

THE ROYAL YACHT *BRITANNIA*

In 1953 the ocean-going Royal Yacht *Britannia* was launched on Clydebank. She remained in service for over 40 years, travelling more than a million miles to every corner of the world on voyages that included 968 official and state visits, family holidays and royal honeymoons. For the Queen and her family *Britannia* was 'home', a place to work, entertain and relax. Now fully restored and moored at Leith, *Britannia* still contains the fittings, furnishings, paintings and photographs from her working days. Tours start in the visitor centre, where exhibits and film tell the yacht's story. From here visitors follow a route round the yacht with an audio handset, whose soundtrack explains the different areas on show. These include the bridge, the Queen's bedroom and sitting room, the splendid dining room, the decks and the engine room.

www.royalyachtbritannia.co.uk

✚ *143 B5* ✉ Ocean Terminal, Leith ☎ 0131 555 5566 🕐 Apr–Sep daily 9:30–6; Oct–Mar daily 10–5. Last tours 90 minutes before closing ✋ Expensive 🍴 Café in visitor centre (£–££) 🚌 1, 11, 22, 34, 35, 36 direct from Waverley Bridge ❓ Booking strongly advised

ST MARY'S EPISCOPAL CATHEDRAL

In 1870, the Misses Barbara and Mary Coates, devoted Episcopalians, left a legacy in the shape of land and money for the building of a cathedral in the West End of Edinburgh. St Mary's, with the sisters' 17th-century mansion still in its shadow, is the result, a soaring Victorian Gothic creation that dominates this part of the city. Designed by Sir George Gilbert Scott and built between 1874 and 1879, it is a cruciform church whose central tower rises to 276ft (84m) – the full effect is best seen from Melville Street. The twin western towers were added in 1917, and are affectionately known as Barbara and Mary, in memory of the cathedral's donors. The interior combines architectural sobriety with a pious cosiness; look out for the glowing murals by Phoebe Anna Traquair, a leading figure in the Arts and Crafts movement.

✚ *142 D4* ✉ Palmerston Place ☎ 0131 225 6293 ◷ Daily 7:15–6 (9pm in summer) ♿ Free 🚌 3, 13, 25, 31, 33 ❓ Regular organ recitals and concerts; choral evensong during term time. Phone cathedral for information

THE SCOTTISH NATIONAL GALLERY OF MODERN ART AND THE DEAN GALLERY

An afternoon in Edinburgh's superbly designed and exciting modern art galleries makes a fascinating and stimulating contrast to medieval and Georgian Edinburgh. In 1999 Edinburgh's permanent exhibition space for modern art doubled with the opening of the Dean Gallery. The two galleries lie on either side of Belford Road, the Gallery of Modern Art housed in a 19th-century neoclassical former school, the Dean in an earlier ex-hospital. The Gallery of Modern Art has a fine collection of international and Scottish 20th-century art, with examples of Fauvism, Expressionism, and Surrealism. Look out for works by Francis Bacon and Jackson Pollock. Across the road, the Dean contains Edinburgh's Dada and Surrealist collection, as well as many works by Eduardo Paolozzi, the Scottish sculptor whose work you may also have seen in the Museum of Scotland (➤ 36–37).

www.nationalgalleries.org.uk

✚ *142 D4* ✉ Belford Road ☎ 0131 624 6200 ◷ Fri–Wed 10–5, (till 6am during Festival) ♿ Free 🍴 Café in Gallery of Modern Art (£–££), Café Newton in Dean Gallery (£) 🚌 13, free bus links all five national galleries ❓ Charges for special exhibitions

STOCKBRIDGE

Situated at the bottom of the slopes of New Town, the lively residential district of Stockbridge was once a milling and tanning village lying alongside the Water of Leith (▶ 113) and was the access point for livestock entering the city. In 1786 the present stone bridge was built and over the next 100 years Stockbridge gradually merged with Edinburgh as the tenement buildings, trim terraces and genteel villas went up. By the 1970s the area was crumbling, ripe for students, artists and the first alternative lifestylers, who moved in attracted by the low rents. In their wake came shops and restaurants, gentrification followed and Stockbridge once more became a desirable place to live. It's an alluring mélange of smart and cosy, where traditional foodshops rub shoulders with trendy bars and designer outlets. Make for St Stephen's Street to get a lingering taste of 1970s Stockbridge, before heading along the water's edge-footpath to explore the Water of Leith.

➕ *142 C4* ✉ Stockbridge 🚌 23, 27, 29, 36

SWANSTON

Driving is the simplest way to get to Swanston, perhaps the prettiest of all Edinburgh's 'villages' and barely part of the city at all. Separated from the urban sprawl by the southern bypass and lying on the slopes of the Pentlands, the middle of this conservation village has changed little since the 19th century. A group of thatched cottages clusters round the village green together with the original 18th-century farmhouse and old school. Swanston is best known for its links with author Robert Louis Stevenson; he came to spend the summers here with his family and nurse from 1867 to 1880.

✚ *142 F4* ✉ Swanston 🚌 5, 17, 27 followed by walk

THE WATER OF LEITH

The Water of Leith runs for more than 20 miles (32km) through a string of suburbs and Edinburgh itself to reach the Firth of Forth at Leith. Most of its course is a gentle meander, with more dramatic scenery at Dean (➤ 104), where the water has carved its way through a deep gorge. For hundreds of years the banks were lined with mills, with up to 80 on the bottom stretch in the early 1800s. A walkway (13 miles/21km) follows the path of the

river from Balerno to Leith, a good way to explore the area. The nicest stretch by far is focused around Stockbridge (➤ 112); this agreeable walk (➤ 114–115) gives access upriver to the Scottish National Gallery of Modern Art (➤ 111) and downstream to the Royal Botanic Garden (➤ 46–47). Alternatively, follow the last stages of the Water through Leith, where you'll see some 17th- and 18th-century warehouses and merchants' houses near the Water's end at the docks.

✚ *142 D3* ✉ Runs from Balerno to Leith with access at different points 🚌 Balerno 44; Leith 10, 11, 22, 36

ℹ 24 Lanark Road (near Balerrno) ☎ 0131 455 7367 🕐 Daily 10–4 🚌 44

a walk through the Water of Leith

*From Queensferry Street turn left
steeply down Bell's Brae to join the
Water of Leith Walkway in Dean Village.*

This is a good opportunity to explore the
village (➤ 104).

*Walk downstream, under the soaring
Dean Bridge to reach St Bernard's Well.*

This elegant columned temple, with its
statue of the Roman goddess Hygeia,
marks the sulphurous mineral springs of
St. Bernard's Well, discovered by three
schoolboys in the 1760s. It quickly became
popular as a place of healing. The wellhouse was designed
by Alexander Nasmyth in 1789.

*Turn left and cross the river, then right down Dean
Terrace to the centre of Stockbridge (➤ 112). Cross
Deanhaugh Street and rejoin the riverside path. Continue
to Bridge Place, then cross the road and turn right up
Arboretum Avenue. As the river curves, turn right along
Rocheid Path.*

You are now opposite the rows
of streets known as The Colonies
(➤ 101).

*Follow the path down Inverleith
Terrace Lane and turn left into
Inverleith Row. After 200yds (183m)
turn left to enter the Royal Botanic
Garden (➤ 46–47) and walk*

through by whichever route you like to Arboretum Place on the west side of the gardens. Cross the road and walk straight through Inverleith Park to Fettes Avenue.

The soaring and ornate building in front of you is Fettes College, the school where the former prime minister, Tony Blair, was educated.

Turn left down Fettes Avenue and continue, then turn left at the junction with Comely Bank Road, which becomes Raeburn Place.

Distance 3 miles (4.8km)
Time 1.5 hours walking; 2–2.5 with visit to Royal Botanic Garden
Start Point Queensferry Street 🚩 136 D1 🚌 13, 19, 29, 37, 41
End Point Raeburn Place 🚩 136 A1 🚌 19, 24, 29, 42
Lunch The Terrace Café (£) ✉ Royal Botanical Garden, Inverleith Row ☎ 0131 552 0616

Excursions

Using Edinburgh as a base, it's possible to get a real taste of the diversity of Scotland – its spectacular scenery, dramatic coastline, forbidding castles and grand mansions, attractive villages and ancient towns. Within a few hours' drive, north or south, you can experience a wealth of different sights, which do much to put the city into perspective as the country's capital.

Central Scotland is home to the majority of Scots, with good roads and transport links, much of Scotland's industry and an increasing sense of purpose and hope for the future. Equally, some of the country's best agricultural land lies near at hand, while the hills, lochs and rivers offer the chance to appreciate a sense of space. Glasgow's dynamism stands in contrast to the tranquillity of the Fife and Borders villages, while its rich cultural life and history are further assets which will add to your Edinburgh experience.

GLASGOW

Glasgow, Scotland's largest city, lies a mere 50 miles (80km) from Edinburgh, a city so different in heritage, atmosphere and style that it might as well be ten times the distance. Industrial Glasgow, decaying 40 years ago, is now one of Britain's most go-ahead cities, with superb 19th-century architecture and a tangible atmosphere of dynamism. Go there to enjoy the contrast with Edinburgh, the buzz of its designer stores, restaurants and museums, and the wonderful friendliness of its people.

www.seeglasgow.com

✚ *143 inset map B6* ✉ 45 miles (73km) from Edinburgh
ℹ 11 George Square ☎ 0141 204 4400;
Airport Tourist Information Centre, Glasgow
International Airport, Paisley ☎ 0141 848 4440

Burrell Collection

Glasgow inherited Sir William Burrell's outstanding art collections in 1944, but it was not until 1983 that a suitable home was built for them, a clean-lined stone-and-glass structure in Pollok Country Park on the south side of the city. Here you'll find paintings, furniture, sculpture and ceramics, architectural fragments and superb Egyptian, Greek, Roman and Asiatic pieces of all sorts. Art-lovers journey to Glasgow specifically to see the collection, so you need to allow plenty of

time. The highlight is the huge Warwick Vase, a 2nd-century Roman marble urn on display in the courtyard.

www.glasgowmuseums.com

✉ 2060 Pollokshaws Road, Pollok Country Park ☎ 0141 287 2550
🕐 Mon–Thu, Sat 10–5, Fri, Sun 11–5 🖐 Free 🍴 Restaurant and café (£–££)
🚉 Pollokshaws West (10 mins walk) 🚌 First Bus 45, 47, 48, 57

Charles Rennie Mackintosh Trail

Fans of Glasgow's most famous architect, born here in 1868, can track down some of the best examples of his work, stylistically an entirely original blend of Arts and Crafts, art nouveau and Scottish. Head for the Glasgow School of Art, still a working school and one of his best-known designs, before taking in the famous Willow Tea Rooms in Sauchiehall Street and Bellahouston Park's House for an Art Lover. Kelvingrove Museum and The Hunterian Museum each contain Mackintosh interiors, furniture and decorative objects.

❓ Mackintosh tours are organized by the Charles Rennie Mackintosh Society, Queens Cross Church, 870 Garscube Road ☎ 0141 946 6600

George Square

Glasgow's grandiose George Square epitomizes the city's 19th-century industrial prosperity. Its wide expanse is dominated by the massive block of the magnificent City Chambers, which has an Italian Renaissance-style façade that gives a taste of the wonders within. Sir Walter Scott looms over it all from a 79ft (24m) column, and 10 other statues include those of Queen Victoria, Robert Burns and James Watt. Southeast from the square spreads the 'Merchant City', once the focus of trading, now a booming area of chic bars and designer stores.

✉ George Square 🍽 Range of restaurants, bars and cafés (£–£££)
🚇 Buchanan Street

People's Palace

There's no better place to get a feel for the social history of Glasgow than in the 1898 People's Palace, which has exhibitions devoted to all aspects of everyday and working life in the city. The museum displays are interactive and visitor-friendly. The splendid adjoining Winter Gardens were badly damaged by a fire in 1998.

✉ Glasgow Green ☎ 0141 271 29 62 🕐 Mon–Thu, Sat 10–5, Fri, Sun 11–5
🎟 Free 🚌 First Bus 16, 18, 40, 61, 62, 64, 263

HADDINGTON

Set in the fertile land between the Lammermuir Hills and the coast, the royal burgh of Haddington has no less than 130 buildings listed as being of historical or architectural interest, a fine late medieval parish church, a beguilingly odd-shaped square as well as galleries, museums and enticing shops. Don't miss the alabaster Elizabethan monuments in the Lauderdale Aisle in St Mary's Church, which also houses the tomb of Jane Carlyle, wife of the historian Thomas Carlyle. Outside town, **Lennoxlove House,** seat of the Dukes of Hamilton, is one of Scotland's grandest houses, with historical relics and fine furniture, paintings and porcelain.

✚ *143 inset map A8* ✉ 20 miles (32km) from Edinburgh

Lennoxlove House

✉ Lennoxlove, Haddington ☎ 01620 823720 ⊘ Easter–Oct Wed, Thu, Sat 2–4:30 ✋ Moderate

LINLITHGOW

Visitors to Linlithgow should head first to the **Linlithgow Story,** which relates the history of this medieval industrial area and royal burgh. Today the **Linlithgow Palace** is the main draw, a well-preserved lochside ruin, where Mary, Queen of Scots was born in 1542. Next door stands St Michael's Church, rebuilt in 1424 and topped by an eye-catching aluminium tower in the 1960s. The town is liberally dotted with fine 17th-century buildings, while outside stands the House of the Binns, a 17th-century house bridging the architectural gap between fortified stronghold and mansion.

✚ *143 inset map A7* ✉ 18 miles (29km) from Edinburgh

Linlithgow Palace

☎ 01506 842896; www.historic-scotland.gov.uk ⏰ Apr–Sep daily 9:30–5:30; Oct–Mar 9:30–4:30 ✋ Moderate

The Linlithgow Story

✉ 143 High Street ☎ 01506 670677; www.linlithgowstory.org.uk
⏰ Easter–Oct Mon–Sat 11–5, Sun 1–4

NORTH BERWICK

North Berwick, once a fishing and trading port, is now a prosperous commuter town and holiday resort, with solid Victorian buildings, a bustling harbour, a renowned golf course, good shops, and sandy beaches and impressive coastline nearby. If you want something more energetic than a beach stroll you could tackle Berwick Law, the 614ft (187m) volcanic rock formation behind the town. Birdwatchers should head for the **Scottish Seabird Centre,** where you can see, study and learn more about the birds of the Bass Rock and of the surrounding coastline.

➕ *143 inset map A8* ✉ 26 miles (41km) from Edinburgh

Scottish Seabird Centre

✉ North Berwick Harbour ☎ 01620 890202; www.seabird.org ⏱ Feb–Mar and Oct Mon–Fri 10–5, Sat–Sun 10–5:30; Nov–Jan Mon–Fri 10–4, Sat–Sun 10–5:30 ✋ Expensive 🚌 First Bus 124

Dirleton

Near the shores of the Firth of Forth, Dirleton, with its cottages and flower-crammed gardens, clusters around its village green with the ruins of an ancient **castle** rising to one side. Built in the 13th century, the castle was repeatedly rebuilt on its natural rock platform until its final destruction in 1650. Today, it's one of the area's most romantic ruins, enhanced by its lovely gardens, first recorded in the 16th century.

➕ *143 inset map A8*

Dirleton Castle

✉ Dirleton, 3 miles (4.5km) from North Berwick ☎ 01620 850330 ⏱ Apr–Sep daily 9:30–5:30; Oct–Mar daily 9:30–4:30 ✋ Moderate 🚌 First Bus 124

Tantallon Castle

The castle at Tantallon stands on a promontory
high above the sea, the entire headland
protected by massive walls and earthworks.
Behind, a spectacular exposed coastal
view opens up, with the Bass Rock in the
background. One of Scotland's most evocative
ruins, Tantallon was built in the 14th century
as an enclosure castle, and is little more than
walls, towers and defences 'enclosing' a grassy
platform on the cliffs above the pounding sea.
Built of local red rock, its 50ft (15m) thick walls
are flanked by towers and pierced by a central
gatehouse-keep. The stronghold was besieged
and blockaded several times and passed in and
out of the Douglas family's ownership down the
years. In 1651 it was attacked by English forces
under the command of General Monk, and its
medieval defences proved no match for state-
of-the-art 17th-century ordnance.

✚ *143 inset map A8* ✉ 2.6 miles (4.2km) from North
Berwick ☎ 01620 892727 🕒 Apr–Sep daily 9:30–5:30;
Oct–Mar Sat–Wed 9:30–4:30 💷 Moderate

PEEBLES

Long popular with visitors, Peebles is a clean and couthy (friendly) riverside town beautifully set beside the Tweed and girdled with rolling hills. Antiquities include two ancient churches, a 14th-century Mercat Cross and a graceful five-arched bridge, first built in the 15th century. The town has been a wool-manufacturing base for many years, and has plenty of wool and knitwear shops and some interesting antiques shops. The town's literary connections are strong; William and Robert Chambers, the founders of Chambers Dictionary, were born here, Robert Louis Stevenson lived here as a child, and John Buchan, author of *The Thirty-Nine Steps*, spent summers here with his family.

➕ *143 inset map B7* ✉ 26.6 miles (38km) from Edinburgh

ℹ High Street ☎ 0870 6080404 🕐 Mon–Sat 10–5, Sun 10–2

Neidpath Castle

It's a pleasant walk from the middle of Peebles to Neidpath Castle, an imposing turreted structure gloriously set on a rocky outcrop above a bend of the River Tweed. This 14th-century L-plan tower house has passed from the Frasers via the Hays, Douglases and Scotts to the Earls of Wemyss, who restored it in the 19th century. Children enjoy exploring the castle with its pit prison and small museum, and you can picnic in the grounds.

www.neidpathcastle.co.uk

➕ *143 inset map B7* ✉ Peebles ☎ 01721 720333 🕐 Easter weekend and May–Sep Wed–Sat 10:30–5, Sun 12:30–5 🦽 Moderate

ROSSLYN CHAPEL

For a glimpse of some of Britain's finest medieval stone carving head for Rosslyn Chapel, well known to readers of *The Da Vinci Code* by Dan Brown. Founded in 1447 by William Sinclair, the 3rd Earl of Orkney, the chapel was intended to form part of a huge collegiate church dedicated to St Michael, which was never built. Only 69ft (21m) long, the entire chapel is profusely carved with intricate and sophisticated sculptures, entwined with flowers and

foliage. Most famous is the so-called Prentice Pillar, said to have been carved by an apprentice while his master was away; so fine was the pupil's work that his master killed him out of jealousy on his return.

www.rosslynchapel.org.uk

➕ *143 inset map B7* ✉ Roslin, Midlothian, 8.5 miles (14km) from Edinburgh
☎ 0131 440 2159 🕐 Apr–Sep Mon–Sat 9:30–6, Sun 12–4:45; Oct–Mar
Mon–Sat 9:30–5, Sun 12–4:45 💷 Expensive

Index

Acknowledgements

The Automobile Association would like to thank the following photographers, companies and picture libraries for their assistance in the preparation of this book.

Abbreviations for the picture credits are as follows – (t) top; (b) bottom; (c) centre; (l) left; (r) right; (AA) AA World Travel Library.

4l Taxi, Edinburgh Inspiring Capital; **4c** Edinburgh Castle, AA/R Elliott; **4r** Victoria Street, Edinburgh Inspiring Capital; **5l** Linlithgow Palace, AA/K Paterson; **5c** Snowsport Centre, Edinburgh Inspiring Capital; **5r** Arthur's Seat, AA/K Paterson; **6** Rosslyn Chapel, AA/M Alexander; **7** Balmoral Hotel, AA/R Elliott; **8** Fireworks, AA/J Smith; **9** Window, St Giles, AA/K Paterson; **10** Military tattoo, AA/J Smith; **11** St Bernard's Well, AA; **12/13** Thistle, AA/E Ellington; **14** Palace of Holyroodhouse, AA/J Smith; **15** Greyfriar's Bobby, AA/K Paterson; **16** Taxi, Edinburgh Inspiring Capital; **22** Waverley Station, Edinburgh Inspiring Capital; **24** Taxi, Edinburgh Inspiring Capital; **27** Postbox, Edinburgh Inspiring Capital; **30/31** View from Calton Hill, AA/R Elliott; **32/33** Salisbury Crags, AA/J Smith; **34** Edinburgh Castle, AA/J Beazley; **34/35** Fireworks, AA; **35** Robert the Bruce, AA/J Smith; **36/37** Museum of Scotland, AA/K Paterson; **37** Museum of Scotland interior, Edinburgh Inspiring Capital; **38/39** Busts, AA/K Paterson; **39tl** National Gallery of Scotland, AA/K Paterson; **39br** National Gallery of Scotland exterior, Edinburgh Inspiring Capital; **40** New Town door, AA/J Smith; **41** New Town, Edinburgh Inspiring Capital; **42** Our Dynamic Earth detail, Edinburgh Inspiring Capital; **42/43** Our Dynamic Earth, Edinburgh Inspiring Capital; **44** Lantern, AA/D Corrance; **44/45t** Gate detail, AA/J Smith; **44/45b** Palace of Holyroodhouse, AA/J Smith; **46** Entrance gate, AA/I Love; **46/47** Lily pond, AA/K Paterson; **47** Sign, AA/I Love; **48** Gladstone's Land, AA/J Smith; **49tl** Back of Royal Mile, AA/J Smith; **49br** Deacon Brodies' Tavern, AA/J Smith; **50** Walter Scott, AA/S Whitehorne; **51** Scott Monument, Edinburgh Inspiring Capital; **52/53** Victoria Street, Edinburgh Inspiring Capital; **55** The Hub, AA/K Paterson; **56** Camera Obscura, AA/K Paterson; **57** Camera Obscura sign, AA/K Paterson; **58/59** Edinburgh Exchange, AA/J Smith; **60/61** The Hub, AA/K Paterson; **61** Gladstone's Land, AA/K Paterson; **62/63** Grassmarket, Edinburgh Inspiring Capital; **64/65** The Meadows, Edinburgh Inspiring Capital; **66/67b** Parliament Square, AA/K Paterson; **66/67t** West Parliament Square, AA/K Paterson; **68/69** Stained glass window, AA/J Smith; **69tr** St Giles cathedral, AA/J Smith; **69bl** Scotch Whisky Heritage Centre, AA/K Paterson; **70** Victoria Street, AA/J Smith; **71** Victoria Street, AA/K Paterson; **72** Canongate Tolbooth, AA/J Smith; **73** Holyrood Park, AA/K Paterson; **74** Holyrood Abbey, AA/K Paterson; **76tl** John Knox's House, AA/J Smith; **76/77** John Knox's House, AA; **77tr** Museum of Childhood, AA/K Paterson; **78** Model in regimental dress, AA/K Paterson; **79** The People's Story, AA/K Paterson; **80/81** Scottish Parliament, Adam Elder/Scottish Parliament; **82** Pipe Band, Edinburgh Inspiring Capital; **83** Skyline, Edinburgh Inspiring Capital; **85** Calton Hill, Edinburgh Inspiring Capital; **86** New Town, AA/J Smith; **86/87** Charlotte Square, AA/J Smith; **88/89** The Georgian House, AA/K Paterson; **89cr** The Mound, AA/K Paterson; **90/91** Princes Street, AA/J Smith; **92** Ross fountain, AA/J Smith; **92/93** Royal Scottish Academy, AA/K Paterson; **94cl** Home of Robert Louis Stevenson, AA/K Paterson; **94/95** New Town, Edinburgh Inspiring Capital; **95tl** Scott Monument, AA/J Smith; **95br** Princes Street Gardens, AA/J Smith; **96/97** Scottish National Portrait Gallery, AA/K Paterson; **98** Water of Leith, Edinburgh Inspiring Capital; **99** Water of Leith, Edinburgh Inspiring Capital; **100/101** View from Braid Hills, AA/K Paterson; **101bl** The Colonies, AA/K Paterson; **102/103** Craigmillar Castle, AA; **103bl** Cramond, AA/K Paterson; **104** Dean village, AA/K Paterson; **105** Duddingston, Edinburgh Inspiring Capital; **106/107** Edinburgh Zoo, AA/D Corrance; **107br** Leith, AA/K Paterson; **108cl** Murrayfield Stadium, AA/K Paterson; **108/109** Royal Scottish Observatory, AA/K Paterson; **110** Royal Yacht Britannia, AA/K Paterson; **112tl** Stockbridge, Edinburgh Inspiring Capital; **112/113** Swanston, AA/D Corrance; **114tr** St Bernard's Well, AA; **114bl** Stockbridge, AA/K Paterson; **115** Dean Village, AA/K Paterson; **116/117** Linlithgow Palace, AA/K Paterson; **119** The Burrell Collection, AA/S Whitehorne; **120** House for an Art Lover, AA/S Whitehorne; **122/123** Linlithgow Palace, AA/K Paterson; **124/125** Dirleton Castle gardens, AA/K Paterson; **125br** Tantallon Castle, AA/K Paterson; **126/127** Neidpath Castle, AA/M Taylor; **128/129** Rosslyn Chapel, AA/R Elliott.

Every effort has been made to trace the copyright holders, and we apologise in advance for any accidental errors. We would be happy to apply the corrections in the following edition of this publication.

Maps

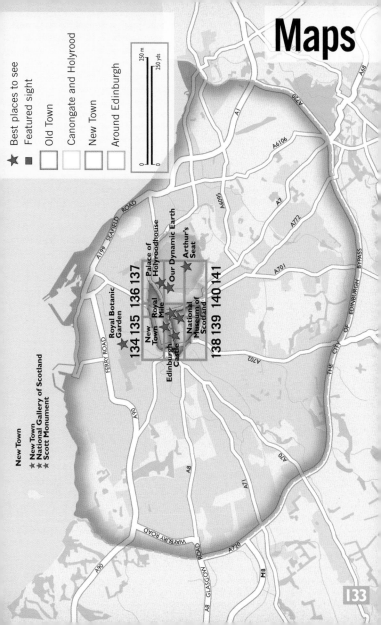

Best places to see
★ Featured sight

- Old Town
- Canongate and Holyrood
- New Town
- Around Edinburgh

250 m
250 yds

New Town
★ New Town
★ National Gallery of Scotland
★ Scott Monument

Royal Botanic Garden

Palace of Holyroodhouse
Our Dynamic Earth
Arthur's Seat

New Town
Royal Mile

National Museum of Scotland

Edinburgh Castle

134 135 136 137

138 139 140 141

A199 SEAFIELD ROAD
FERRY ROAD
A90
A8 GLASGOW ROAD
WARDURY ROAD
A71
A720
A70
M8
THE CITY OF EDINBURGH BYPASS
A702
A701
A772
A7
A1
A6095
A6106
A68
A720

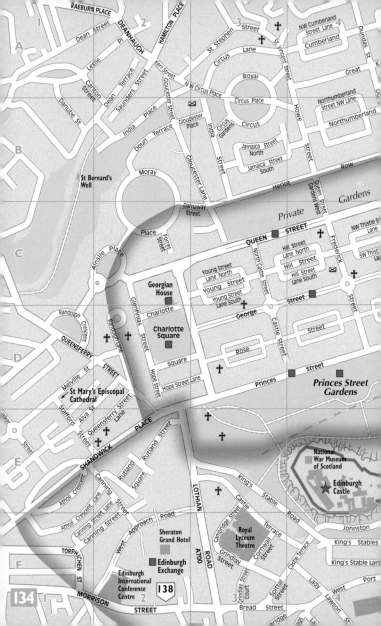

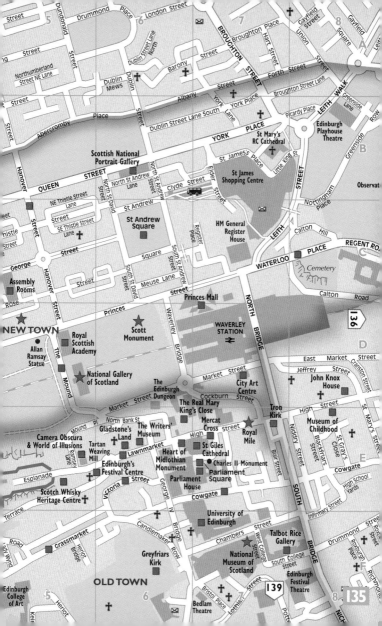

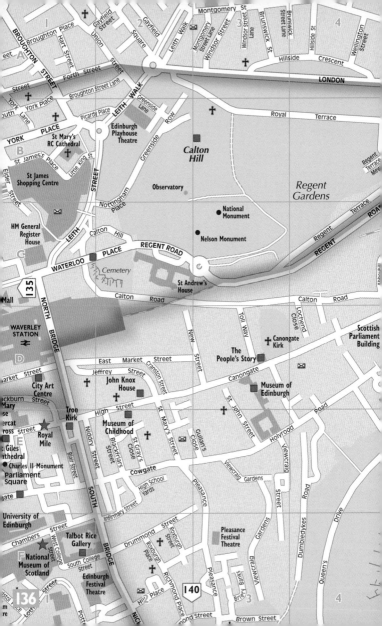

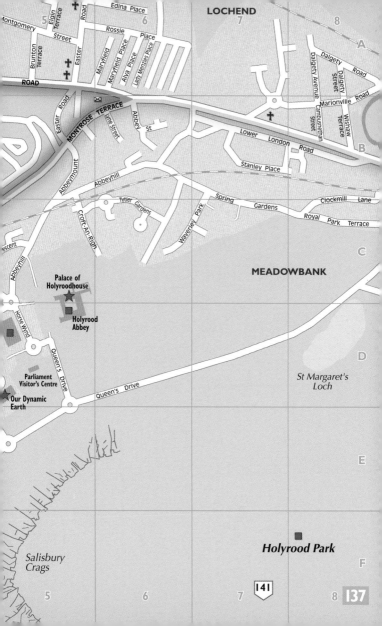

LOCHEND

MEADOWBANK

Palace of
Holyroodhouse

Holyrood
Abbey

St Margaret's
Loch

Parliament
Visitor's Centre

Our Dynamic
Earth

*Salisbury
Crags*

Holyrood Park

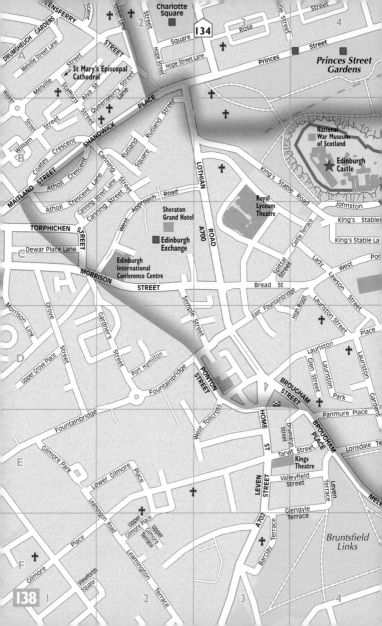

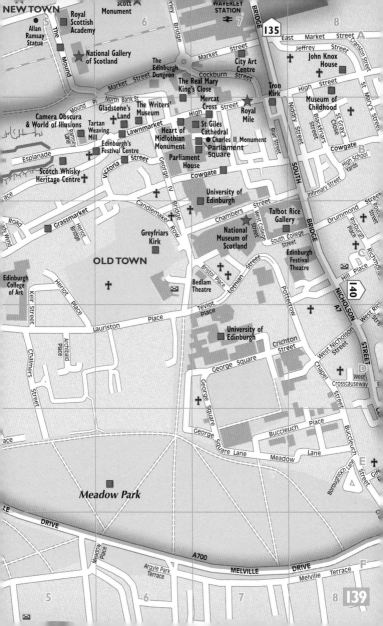

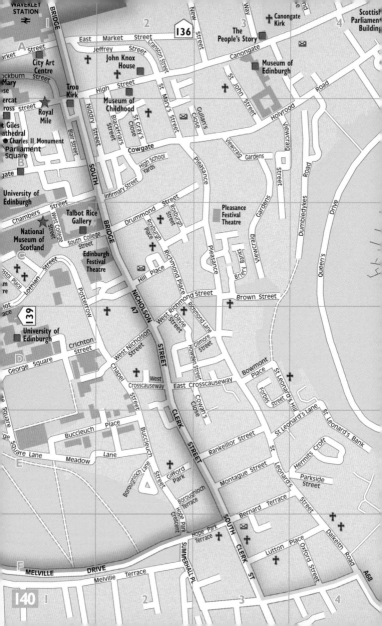

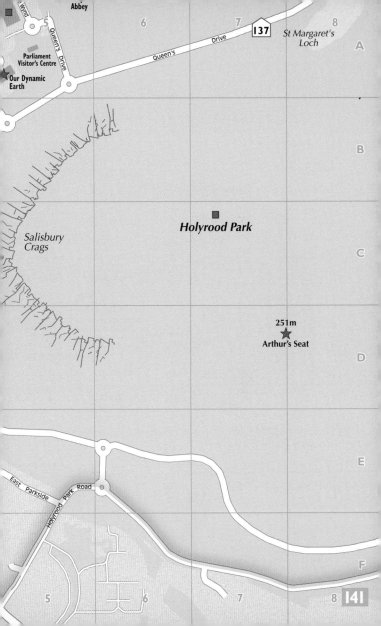

Abbey

137 St Margaret's Loch

Queen's Drive

Queen's Drive

Parliament
Visitor's Centre

★ Our Dynamic
Earth

Salisbury
Crags

■ *Holyrood Park*

251m
★
Arthur's Seat

East Parkside

Holyrood Park Road

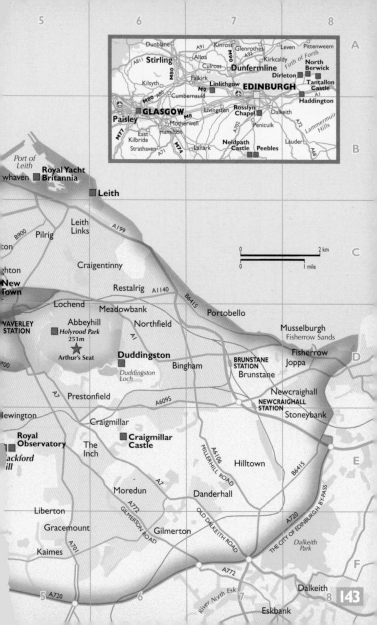

A

Dunblane
A91 Kinross Leven Pittenweem
Alloa Glenrothes
Stirling Kirkcaldy North
Culross Dunfermline Firth of Forth Berwick
Kilsyth Falkirk Dirleton
Linlithgow Tantallon
Cumbernauld EDINBURGH Castle
Haddington
GLASGOW Livingston Rosslyn Dalkeith A1
Paisley Chapel
Motherwell Penicuik Lammermuir
East Hamilton Hills
Kilbride Neidpath Lauder
Strathaven Lanark Castle Peebles
B

Port of
Leith
haven Royal Yacht
Britannia
Leith

Leith
B900 Links A199
Pilrig
ton
Leith
Craigentinny C
ghton
New
Town
Restalrig A1140 B6415
Lochend Portobello
Meadowbank
WAVERLEY Abbeyhill Northfield Musselburgh
STATION Holyrood Park Fisherrow Sands
251m
00 Arthur's Seat Duddingston Fisherrow
Joppa D
Bingham BRUNSTANE
Duddingston STATION
Loch Brunstane
Prestonfield A6095 NEWCRAIGHALL Newcraighall
A7 STATION
Craigmillar Stoneybank
ewington A6095
Royal Craigmillar
Observatory Castle Millerhill road Hilltown E
lackford The Inch B6415
ill
Moredun A7
Liberton Danderhall A720
Gracemount Old Dalkeith Road THE CITY OF EDINBURGH BY-PASS
Gilmerton Road Gilmerton Dalkeith
Kaimes Park
A701
A720 A772 F
River North Esk Dalkeith
Eskbank

143

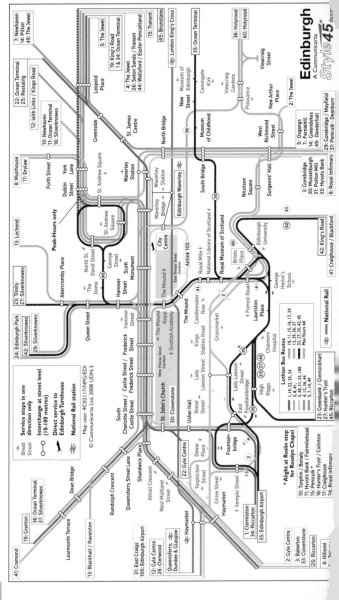

144